THE ENGLISH
COUNTRYMAN

CONTENTS

LIST OF ILLUSTRATIONS

INTRODUCTION

The English Countryman: his life and work A.D. 1500–1900

Other people's lives are always romantic. It does not matter if they live in distant countries or if they lived long ago. Far away and long ago are the spice of the tales we like. The story of the age of chivalry, when the Black Prince was doing daring deeds on the fields of France, when English knights and English archers were winning great victories abroad, is romantic, but as in all wars most of the people stayed at home and lived their ordinary lives.

It is of these ordinary people that this book will try to tell the story. It will try to tell how they lived, and what they lived on, and how their living conditions changed as time passed. For many years now historians have been studying just how those things made up the lives of the ordinary everyday people. One thing is very important. To understand the England of hundreds of years ago we must forget the England of today.

Even so short a time as fifty years ago, when I was a little boy, living in the country, or a little later when I went on cycling tours as a young man, the countryside looked very different from what it is today. There were no tarmac roads then, and the country lanes were deep wallows of mud in winter, very dusty in summer. The only way to get about was on foot, on horseback, or in a trap or carriage, until the railway was reached. When a short journey on the local railway was undertaken it was often very uncomfortable. Most people were not travellers, and many people lived their whole lives in the villages where they were born.

Hundreds of years before the difference was much greater, though the greatest changes have been made in the last 200 years. The main thing to forget is this industrial England where most of the people work in factories, mines, workshops, wholesale and retail shops in the towns. There was none of all this in Tudor times. For one thing there was not then one-tenth of the people now living in the whole country. The whole population of the kingdom was not more than one-half the present-day population of London only, perhaps 4,500,000 at the most, and very likely less than that.

Nearly everybody lived in tiny villages; some in hamlets of only a few families. Most of these villages were situated in a belt of country stretching across the middle of England, bounded by a line from the Wash to the Thames in the east, another from the Wash to the Severn in the north, and the Thames in the south. Very few people lived in the rest of the country. There was the great waste of the Fens in the east, the solitude of the mountains in the north, the great forests of the midland counties; the forest and Weald of Kent, Surrey and Sussex; Windsor Forest in Berkshire practically joined the New Forest in the south; the solitude of the Downs stretched in two great ranges across country from Kent to Cornwall, and from Lincoln to Somerset; all this was nearly empty country, yet to be settled and reclaimed.

England was pretty well settled only in a restricted district, and people lived in the same place as their fathers had done before them. Life was lived according to tradition. People knew the routine of old though they had begun to write it down to prevent disputes.

The life-long villager of today is the exception. In Tudor times almost everyone was a villager; 90 per cent of the population were born, lived out their lives and died in the tiny communities. The size of these villages naturally varied. Some were a little larger, some smaller, and some quite tiny, especially in the wild parts of the country where settlements were only slowly being made. A typical village in the Midlands would be one of 300, 400 or perhaps 500 inhabitants, and these villagers would most likely make up from forty to sixty families, closely related by blood and marriage. Elsewhere in the country the villages were smaller and more scattered.

These people lived much to themselves. Local roads and lanes did not encourage travel. The roads were mere dirt tracks, a sea of mud in winter and a heap of dust in summer: and they did not run between the familiar hedge and ditch of southern England, nor the dry stone walls of Wales and the north. These hedges, ditches and walls had not yet been made. Few people cared to or could travel farther than the next village, and indeed there was little reason for them to do so, for it was only another place much the same as their own. But like us village people were quite pleased to see a stranger or a different place. The market or the fair at the nearest town was the main reason for travelling, and many people could not even manage that short infrequent journey. It was thought a happy thing for a man to be born and live in the same place, and to die there after a placid life of the normal routine of country doings.

The scenery, too, was widely different from what it is today. The open arable fields were much larger than our enclosed fields. Supposing there were forty families in a fairly large village, say 500 people of all ages, they would need an average of, at the very least, five bushels of grain each to keep them for a year, and yields were then very low, usually not more than sixteen bushels of wheat an acre; so 250 acres must be sown each year to feed them, and fifty more to provide seed for the next year.

If the village arable was divided into three fields, there were then 900 acres in all, 300 in each field, and as wise men must provide against the chance of bad luck, there was most likely a little margin over mere necessity. Except for the temporary fences round the growing crop (and these were not universal) all this land was a wide expanse of open country containing a couple of square miles ranged round the village. If there was a stream or river, the meadows on its banks were another open space. Beyond these and the arable stretched the wastes on all sides, usually no more than heath, broom, bramble, and birch on the lighter soils, scrub oak on the clay, and beech forest on much of the chalk hills. All of it was grazed, though a good deal of it must have been strange country to most of the people. It formed the wild wood of the romances, of such romantic writers as William Morris and Jeffery Farnol, and was a very real thing. The land was largely an empty land with its few inhabitants clinging together like the first tiny settlements in some newly discovered colony.

We have already described the life and work of the women who cared for their families during the four centuries from Tudor to Victorian times in our book *The English Countrywoman*. Here we have tried to describe the life and work of their husbands and sons in the fields and at home. Many political and economic changes took place during this long time. These have only been touched upon when they influenced the lives of the men of the land. The men of the land themselves were responsible for great changes. They improved their tools and invented new ones. They adopted new crops and manures. They devised new ways of draining their land. Some improved their houses.

Old customs vanished and new ones took their place. These things constitute the life of the men of the land. Changes there have been, but the procession of the seasons, the processes involved in growing crops and breeding livestock are the same as they always were. Within the framework of these immutable conditions the men of the land have always worked and lived, and it is their personal story that we have attempted in this book.

CHAPTER ONE

The Tudor Farmer

THE TIMES and seasons of farming have not changed in the past 400 years, perhaps not in the last 4,000. Our Tudor ancestors, who farmed the countryside under Henry VII, Henry VIII and his son and daughters, sowed their wheat in the autumn like we do, and their barley in the spring. They harvested both these crops in the summer months as we must.

Like us, too, they turned out their cattle to feed on the spring flush of grass in late April or in May. Calves were then timed to be born in the spring. The poets sang about the happiness of the shepherds and the gambols of the lamb in that season of the year.

Besides sowing and harvest, preparing the seed bed and all the other farm jobs were done in much the same way as we do them, but with simpler tools and without fertilizers. The ox-team or the horse-team dragged the plough, the harrows and the roller if the farmer had one. Clod-breaking was often done by hand; so was weeding and most other jobs. The Tudor farmer's processes were slow, his resources meagre and his yields correspondingly small. His cattle were less productive than ours, and his livelihood much smaller.

Though his daily work was so similar to that of a modern farmer, his social circumstances were very different, and were changing with a gathering momentum. The causes of these changes were numerous, and some almost cataclysmic.

15

About a hundred years before the accession of Henry VII the Black Death had devastated the countryside slaying baron, knight and squire, freeman, villein and serf alike. There had been almost equally devastating famines. This mortality, the result of circumstances then quite outside men's control, caused the breakdown of the feudal system. Its shackles were slowly cast off during the next hundred years and by the reign of Elizabeth it was superseded. The noble landlords, too, killed each other off in the Wars of the Roses, and so made way for a new class of landowners with ideas quite different from those of the feudal nobility.

Plague, famine and war had made for the break-up of medieval society and the transfer of land to new owners. These accidents, too, gave new prestige to the tenant farmer, new powers of bargaining with his landlord, and to the labourer some power to change his place and demand higher wages.

The influence of these events was felt in the reign of Henry VII. Men began to turn to a more commercial and profitable system of farming. The action of Henry VIII in seizing the monastic and abbey lands gave yet more impetus to change. Some of these lands the king kept for himself, some he gave away to his courtiers, some he sold. Often those who were given presents, or made purchases sold again. No less than one-fifth of the whole area of the country passed into the hands of new owners within a few years. The new owners were commercially minded men, like those who had become new owners through the disasters of the previous century. All of them wanted to make money out of their estates rather than to consume their produce in supporting small armies of men-at-arms, retainers and personal servants.

Such were the human causes of change. There were agricultural causes as well. Some historians believe that much of the land that had been farmed ever since the Anglo-Saxon and Scandinavian tribes invaded England was worn out by the fourteenth century. They think that the yields of wheat, barley and rye were falling after a thousand years cultivation of the same fields under the same two- or three-course rotation with no fertilization other than the sheep fold and a trifle of stable manure. Consequently it was more profitable to enclose these arable fields, many of which were divided amongst the village farmers on the much described open field system, and to use the land for sheep grazing. The progress of the woollen manufacture and the increasing demand for wool justified that change. It is not really very likely that the modern belief in soil exhaustion and declining yields is true. Experiments carried out at Rothamsted Experimental Station have shown that wheat can be grown on unmanured land without fallowing for seventy years; the yield only falls to twelve bushels an acre. It continues to yield twelve bushels, and would probably do so for a very long time.

Any early Tudor farmer would have been pleased to harvest twelve bushels an acre, though sixteen bushels may not have been unusual in Elizabeth's reign. In addition, broadly speaking, land that was then open field arable, has remained arable ever since Henry VII's day, though not still distributed in open fields. Only a comparatively small area was affected by the Tudor enclosures for pasture farming, and some of this was compensated for by the enclosure and occupation of the waste in such places as Clitheroe, Halifax, and Rossendale.

Over a thousand books and essays are said to have been written about the rights and wrongs of the Tudor enclosures. It would certainly be unwise to add another to them. Enclosures took place from agricultural necessity, as Lord Ernle argued so long after the event and Trow-Smith more recently, or from greed, as Thomas Bastard believed in 1598.

> "Sheep have eat up our meadows and our downs
> Our corn our wood, whole villages and towns,
> Yea, they have eat up many wealthy men,
> Besides widows and orphan children;
> Besides our statutes and our iron laws
> Which they have swallowed down into their maws.
> Till now I thought the proverb did but jest
> Which said a black sheep was a biting beast."

Though a great many men became poorer as a result of all this disturbance in the countryside, many found opportunity to their hand, seized it, and became better off, if not rich. When times are static people remain as they were; when times are disturbed by flood, famine, disease, war or political manœuvres some men see a golden chance and do not fail to take it. They rise from the humblest ranks to the highest, or at the very least from one grade of society to another. By

B

the most painful economy a humble copyholder could gather together a little capital and become a yeoman lease- or freeholder; a yeoman could, and did, rise to the rank of gentleman. All of them alike remained dependent upon their farms or upon farming for their livelihood. Industry and commerce were the occupation of a small minority of the people, and the great nobles, who made up the court, were limited to some sixty families.

The virtues and character of a country gentleman, the class which all right-minded and ambitious men were anxious to join, were those simple moralities that had always been praised by philosophers through-out the ages. He must keep measure in spending; he must "eate within the Tedure". Prodigality in outrageous and costly array must be avoided. Outrageous play and game were anathema. Unless attention was paid to economical and sensible living, the gentleman farmer would very soon find himself becoming poorer instead of richer, and indeed many of them did at last realize the truth of this good advice. A wise young man would take it to heart. One of the best ways of doing so was to "gette a copy of this presente boke", Fitzherbert's *Boke of Husbandrye*, published first in 1523.

This author was not modest. Not only did he suggest that, in order to manage his farm properly, the gentleman should learn the book by rote, but it was so valuable that he ought, "according to the season of the yere, rede to his Servants what chapter he wyll". It contained nothing except the writer's practical experience well proven in the field.

Besides this book the gentleman farmer must be active about the fields. He must rise betime in the morning and go about the farm, especially by the hedges. In his purse he ought to carry a "pair of tables", tablets on which notes could be made. Anything that he noticed that wanted doing he ought to write on them. Any trespassing livestock must be driven off his land. Any of his own that had strayed where they were not wanted, through a gap in a hedge, must be put back in their own place. If there was any standing water in pasture or corn field a note must be made to drain it off. There were many other things that he ought to note.

"For a man alwaye wanderynge or goinge aboute somewhat fyndeth or seeth that is amyse. And as soone as he seeth any such

defaultes, then let hym take out his tables and wryte the defaultes.
And when he cometh home to diner, supper or at nyght, then let
hym call his bayley or heed servante, and soo show hym the defautes,
that they may shortly be amended. And when it is amended, then
let him put it out of his tables."

This was what Fitzherbert himself had done for ten or twelve
years or more. It was a good system of supervision confirmed by the
proverbial wisdom that the master's foot is the best manure. If he
could not write, the farmer was told to "nycke the defautes upon a
stycke, and to shewe his bayley".

People who came to the house, especially if they carried pitchers,
cans, tankards, bottles, bags, wallets, or bushel pokes, must be carefully
watched. It was all too simple for a dishonest servant to fill such re-
ceptacles with his master's goods for a trifling tip. A good servant was a
great treasure and would not stoop to or allow petty thieving of this
kind that was so damaging to his master.

Tudor farmers had to be parsimonious. They had to watch their
expenses much more carefully than a modern person would feel
necessary. The farmer was advised, for example, to estimate whether
the cost of fire and candle-lights were more than the value of the work
being done when sitting by the fireside on a winter evening. If the work
of the man, his wife and servants was not worth more than the food
eaten and the fire and light, then everybody ought to go to bed. If it
was then they could sit still and get on with it. If they decided to go
to bed to save food, fire and light, they could always get up early in
the morning to do the work, an excellent practice that made a man
"hole in body, holer in soul, and rycher in goodes".

Economy, industry and honesty were then, as ever, preached as
the qualities that led to advancement. Nothing was said of the spirit
of adventurous speculation that was a more rapid way of profit or
ruin. This was the spirit that was bringing cargoes of gold and silver
to Europe from America. These precious metals were one factor in
the rise in prices that took place in the sixteenth century of which
Latimer complained in his well-known sermon, about the difference in
times past and times present. It was his first sermon before Edward VI.
He said that his father was a yeoman, tenant of a farm at a rent of
£4 a year. About six men were employed on the farm. A comparatively

large number of livestock was kept, about a hundred sheep and thirty cows, so Latimer, senior, was a substantial man. He was able to give his son what is sometimes called a college education and to marry his daughters off with substantial dowries. He never refused hospitality to a poorer neighbour and he was generous in alms giving. Rents had risen four times since, and the present tenant of the farm paid sixteen pounds for it. This was such a severe tax on the produce of the farm that the new tenant was poverty-stricken. He could not provide a man to fight the Prince's wars, could scarcely maintain himself or his children, and certainly could spare no alms.

This was not an isolated case. Prices and rents alike were rising and the new landlords were making every effort to squeeze the last halfpenny of profit out of their estates. Some of them had pulled down farms and depopulated villages and towns, and there was loud and continuous outcry against this wickedness throughout the Tudor century. Henry VII had forbidden by statute the demolition of any farmhouse that had twenty acres or more attached to it.

Henry himself realized the objections to changing arable land into pasture. The process enabled the more powerful landowners to eject tenants, whose lands had been held on customary tenure of one sort or another, and to absorb their holdings in the demesne. Not all enclosures were made for that purpose, of course. The King did not disapprove of those made to extend the area under tillage and so improve the national resources. Further legislation passed in later reigns tried to restrain the bad effects resulting from an ill-proportioned expansion of sheep-farming but the fall in the price of wool that took place between 1546 and 1561 was altogether more effective. From then corn growing became more profitable, and some land that had gone down to grass was ploughed up again.

The new landlords did not need to live in the same way as their predecessors. Peace reigned in the land. Settled government and artillery made castles useless. The Tudor aristocracy went in for building on a large scale, erecting great country houses like Montacute, or modifying existing buildings like Woburn. They did not need a multitude of armed retainers; indeed they had been specifically forbidden to maintain private armed forces. The military services of the free tenants were not wanted for the same reasons. The customary services of the unfree tenants had nearly all been commuted for money payments,

The free tenants became leaseholders, paying whatever rents could be forced out of them, or continuing their occupation on the basis of a stock and land lease whereby the stock was supplied by the landowner who shared the profits of its use. Copyholders were often held up for increased fines, and if they could not pay them, turned out of their minute holdings. Thereafter they were entirely dependent upon wages. All the circumstances of the Tudor age combined to consolidate an organization of rural society that has lasted for several hundred years, and still exists in a great deal of our countryside. Landlord, tenant and labourer was the stratification of this society.

The whole population of the country was divided into well-defined classes between whom great gulfs yawned although these boundaries were not impassable. Under Elizabeth towards the end of the period the distinctions became more marked. The gentry, who were becoming steadily of more weight and influence in the social organization, were becoming richer. The scale of their expenditure marked them out from the yeomen and the cottagers. As to the comparatively few citizens, some of them were becoming wealthy, and joining the ranks of the *nouveaux riches* on the land just as some yeomen were rising to the rank of gentlemen.

When a yeoman achieved that distinction he became a little sovereign on his own estate, the representative of the central government and the dispenser of justice in the countryside. In spite of all this grandeur it was impossible for him and his family to remain aloof from village life, even had they wished to do so. All the inhabitants of the village, whatever their social station, were intimate, if not always friendly. Each and everyone was well known to all the others. Little could be concealed in such small communities.

The squire, it has been said, was generally regarded with affectionate respect by his yeomen and tenants. "He did not disdain to appear as the village rival; he gave a fat buck to the village bridal; he was the friend and patron of all; the old Hall was the County Court; its owner was neither feared nor dreaded; the young squire led his tenants to the Low Countries; the old knight's daughter was the cynosure of the county and the gem of the Court."

Below the rank of gentleman were yeoman, husbandman and labourer. The position of the yeoman has been discussed at length by

Miss Mildred Campbell. A valuable and succinct contemporary description runs:

> "Yeomen are those, which by our law are called *Legales homines* free men borne English, and may dispend of their owne free land in yearelie revenue, to the summe of fortie shillings sterling (or six pounds as monie goeth in our times). This sort of people have a certaine preheminence, and more estimation than labourers, etc. (the common sort of) artificers, etc. (these) commonlie live wealthelie, keepe good houses and travell to get riches. They are also for the most part farmers to gentlemen . . . with grasing, frequenting of markets, and keeping of servantes (not idle servantes as gentlemen do) but such as yet get both their owne and part of their master's living) do come to great welth, in somuch that manie of them are able and doo buie the land of unthriftie gentlemen, and often setting their sonnes to the schools, to the universities and to the Ines of the courte; or otherwise leaving them sufficient lands whereupon they may live without labour, doo make them by those meanes to become gentlemen."

Bishop Latimer would have found no fault with this description though his father was a tenant and not a freeholder. Like the elder Latimer many other well-to-do tenant farmers were designated yeomen in that age when social structure was so very formal. It could be compared with the universe in its order and stability.

> "The heavens themselves, the planets and this centre
> Observe degree, priority and place."

was the pattern to which human society ought to conform.

In legal theory the yeoman was the forty shilling freeholder, but in practice the term was elastic. Substantial leaseholders were named yeomen in court cases and in wills and other documents. These were farmers who held their land at a fixed rent from a landowner for a definite number of years, or for the lifetime of the tenant and possibly two of his heirs. Still another class was included, the richer copyholder who in Tudor times paid a nominal yearly rent and a fine when the land passed from father to son or to some other person. The term copyholder was given to these men because the transfer of their property from one hand to another was entered in the Court Roll of the Manor, and their title was secured by their copy of that Roll. The poorer copyholders were known as husbandmen, a category that included the occupiers of the numerous minute holdings of an acre or two.

Amongst the farmers there was a ferment of ambitious activity as there was amongst the gentry. Thornbury's idea that the yeoman and the husbandman was content in that state of life to which it had pleased God to call him must now be modified. His sketch is nevetheless worth quoting.

"Rude, but hearty in manner, the Elizabethan farmer was one of a distinctive class strongly divided from either the labourer or the gentleman. He could not pass beyond the boundaries of his class and he did not wish to do it; he could hawk and hunt, attend the fairs, and occasionally visit London, but he never thought of rivalling the lord of the manor. He was generally superstitious and a great respecter of old customs."

It is now certain that the yeoman was not pinned down in his class, the most dynamic in Tudor society, a class that was growing more wealthy and acquiring more land everywhere. Many were rising in the social scale and becoming gentry. Those who did not achieve this distinction were doing well, possibly at the expense of others who failed, grew poorer and sank to the level of day labourers.

The life of these successful men remained simple. Their success was often due more to saving pence than to excessive profit. "The farmer has no Flemish tapestry or Dutch linen"; writes Thornbury, "he drinks from bowls, and has but a plain table board and little plate; his bed is flax, and his curtains are home-spun wool; his coat is of freize or Kendal green; he has two doublets, and not often more than two servants."

Twenty acres had been considered "a competent proportion of land" to provide for a family in the reign of Henry VII. If that acreage was then carefully cultivated it would "of necessity enforce the dweller not to be a beggar or a cottager, but a man of some substance that might keep hinds and servants, and set the plough on going". The maintenance of a large number of farms of not less than that size would provide for a yeomanry or middle people of a condition between gentlemen and cottagers or peasants.

On such a farm a few livestock were kept and grain was grown. Amongst the innumerable inventories of the century wide variations are found. Throughout the sixteenth century and much later an average holding almost anywhere in the country might carry two four-year-old steers, two cows and a heifer, two younger bullocks and two calves, four sheep and two lambs, and a couple of "hog shoots". Poultry was about three hens, two chickens and two geese. Plough irons including a share and a coulter, and a pair of plough wheels, were essential.

Household gear consisted of two or three bedsteads, flock beds and bolsters, coverlets, a few pairs of sheets. A table board (probably a trestle), a form or bench, stools, a chair for the master, brass pots and bowls, a few platters of wood or pewter, a pot-hanger, kettle, frying pan or skillet, a cupboard and a chest, two or three candlesticks. The better off had a tablecloth and napkins.

The goodman's wearing apparel was a gown, doublet, jacket, two pairs of hose, two shirts, a sleeved coat, a freize coat, canvas doublet and a cappe. His wife possessed a best gown and petticoat, two or three kyrtles, an old petticoat, a pair of foresleeves, hose, ribbons, a cappe and ribbons, a smock, a neckerchief and other kerchief, some napkins. A prized possession, doubtless a husband's gift, was a silver pin.

The value of these modest possessions was very small in terms of modern currency. They were set down in inventories at so little as £14 in the beginning of the century. At the end they came to so much as £107, but, of course, the lists of goods, though similar, was not identical in the two documents. There were more things in the second and each item was valued at a higher figure.

These were the possessions of small men. One rich leaseholder died owning stock to the value of over £400. His lease had four years to run at £80 and this was estimated to be worth £320. He was one of hundreds just as wealthy and who were striving continuously to add to their possessions. The rise of the Pastons in eastern England is well known. Similarly the Furses of Mosshead were progressing as rapidly in the west. Many other examples are cited by Miss Campbell.

These people were the farmers. There were great differences between them. Some occupied only tiny holdings, and were little, if any, better off than the day labourers who formed with them "the fourth and last sort of people of England". William Harrison thought of them as in the same social class as retailers who had no land, copyholders (rather incorrectly as is now thought), and tradesmen, like tailors, shoemakers, carpenters, masons and bricklayers.

"This (fourth and last sort of people) therefore have neither voice nor authorities in the common wealth, but are to be ruled, and not to rule other; yet they are not altogether neglected, for in cities and corporat townes, for default of yeomen, they are faine to make up their inquests of such manner of people. And in villages they are commonlie made churchwardens, sidesmen, aleconners (now and then) constable and manie times the name of hedboroughs."

All these members of rural society lived in small village communities. The social classes were quite clearly defined but there was a measure of intimacy between the individuals composing these isolated and self-contained societies that has persisted until almost modern times. The system of parish government had a deal to do with this.

The justices of the peace were the local sovereigns. They appointed the churchwardens, the highway surveyor, the overseer of the poor, and the constable, unpaid offices to which, as Harrison pointed out, all the villagers were liable to be appointed whether they wished to be or not.

The squire, clergy (rector or curate), and the churchwarden and others formed the village hierarchy. The visits of the archdeacon and the bishop made them feel their responsibilities. At every crisis in the villager's life these authorities stepped in.

"They compelled him to attend on specified days his parish church, and no other; to be married there; to have his children baptized and his wife churched there; to receive a certain number of times communion there; to contribute to the maintenance of the church and churchyard, as well as to the finding of requisites for service or the church ornaments or utensils. In his parish church he and his children were catechized and instructed, and, if the latter were taught in a neighbouring school house, it was under the strict supervision of the ordinary and by his or the bishop's license or allowance. So true was this that the schoolmaster was, like the parson, a church officer. For the parishioners his church was the place of business where all local affairs, civil or ecclesiastical, were transacted, as well as the centre of social life in the village . . . he and his fellow warden were held responsible by the official."

This regulation of the villagers' domestic life was similar to the regulation of his professional life by the manorial court, where he could be fined for offences against what we call good husbandry. These courts ordered ditches to be scoured when they were neglected; decided the time when the open field must be fenced against animals; forbade mangy horses or those infected with farcy to be turned out on the commons; saw to it that commoners did not turn out more cattle or sheep than they had a right to; ordered holes dug on the common to be filled up; ordered dunghills to be removed from the common or highway; fined squatters who put up cottages on the waste; prevented strangers from other parishes cutting turf or bracken; controlled the use of water courses for retting hemp and flax; maintained the Lord's pinfold by forced labour. Some elementary attempts at sanitation were made too. At Giggleswick, Yorkshire, villagers were forbidden to steep fish or flesh in the common well.

The constable, elected by rote and unpaid, was responsible for the preservation of law and order in the village, for the apprehension of offenders and haling them before the justice. When necessary he called out the *posse comitatus*, and pursued offenders to the boundaries of the parish, sometimes farther. His post was no sinecure in that hot-blooded and quarrelsome age. Most men carried a knife or dagger, and were prone to use it in a quarrel. If he interfered the constable was as liable to get stabbed as one of the fighters. Indeed he might be and was attacked by the riotous when he attempted to do his duty. Petty crime was rife. Tusser warned his readers not to leave their linen out of sight nor too conveniently to an unwatched door or window. Clothing, pots and pans, loose tools or any other article that could easily be picked up and carried away without much risk of discovery, would mysteriously disappear. There were many poor and necessitous, and there were wandering beggars and vagrants, whose fingers were very sticky. More serious thefts, stealing sheep, cattle and horses, were less numerous but not uncommon. Malicious wounding, assault and battery, beating the constable to prevent him serving a warrant upon a relative, happened frequently. Sometimes a man or woman was murdered. Blackmail by common informers was suffered justly and injustly. Occasionally a constable was indicted for embezzlement. Charges of rape were not unknown.

All these crimes and criminals were the business of the constable and must have occupied a good deal of his time. Only when they left him at leisure could he do his work on his own farm, or work for wages to earn his living. And it was his job to see that the punishments inflicted by the justices were carried out. He must duck the scold in the pond or stream or affix the torturing brank. He must put offenders in the stocks or pillory, or whip them at the cart's tail. At the end of his term of office he must have been a thoroughly unpopular character. Obviously, too, these duties hindered his own proper work, and must often have made it impossible.

The farmer then, as now, found his work continuous throughout the day although he could occasionally find time for rustic pleasures and sports. He rose at cock-crow, said his prayers, and set the servants to work on the jobs he thought necessary. Then he went out, looked over his flocks, and saw that all was well with the plough oxen and the dairy cows. At eleven or twelve he returned to dine, "drinking no wine and leaving tobacco for rich people". In the afternoon he may if literate have read some such book as *Foxe's Martyrs* or Hollinshed's *Chronicles*. The evening he spent talking of courses of husbandry, discussing livestock, the dairy, orchards and poultry, listening to the bailiff's account of the day's events on the farm and in the village, or possibly hearing a miraculous tale of foreign parts told by some transient who was enjoying his hospitality.

Tom Nash, the bitterest of lampooners, has given us a sketch of country life and farmer's pleasures. As a youth he was fond of throwing at the stone or leaping, handsomely rising at the stone or pommade and the bear leap. Sometimes he ran in matches, sometimes practised the Cornish hug, or Norfolk twitch or trippet in wrestlings; sometimes he was all for play with single sword or rapier and dagger, long staff or two-handed glaive. Not unseldom if it were May, the country squire's son would betake himself to the common green, and watch Tib and Tom dancing a measure about the maypole; then he was all for riding, and at fifteen he could make the great horse tread, and trot, and gallop at the ring, leaving caroches (coaches) for aged and impotent people. . . .

Tomorrow perhaps he was angling, or gardening, or snaring birds, or shooting from bush to bush, to keep up his use of the bow; in the evening perhaps on the common green at bowls.

This can only have been the life of the squire and well-to-do farmer, and more particularly of their sons. The small holders, who were the majority, worked as hard as the labourers and had little time for recreation. The labourers or servants were allowed to indulge in games or pastimes only by permission, or in the presence of the master, though everyone was obliged to practise at the bow after he was seven years old.

The continual round of pleasure Tom Nash described was never the lot of a working farmer. All the sports and pastimes in his list might very well be indulged in from time to time and at the proper seasons of the year, but serious application to the business of farming was as necessary, if not more necessary then, as it is today. A modern farmer looks to sales of his produce to get his living; so did a Tudor farmer to some extent. But he also relied upon his harvest for the grain to make his own bread, and upon his dairy for his own milk, butter and cheese, as well as what he could spare for sale. Therefore, he had, willynilly, to be painstaking and exhaustingly industrious if he would eat. Indeed his life was a true reflection of the Biblical condemnation that in the sweat of his face he should eat his bread.

The character of an ideal tenant was clearly recognized by the Elizabethan landlord. The best man to choose was a native of the parish, lusty and strong, who thrived in health upon his natural soil, not too young and well known to the landowner as a good man. He need not be rich. Experience of hard and economic living would make him careful of both his own interests as a farmer and of the landlord's as owner of the property. A man of this sort would naturally be married to a thrifty wife, who would be the mother of healthy and well-cared-for children, trained to help in the work.

The sensible farmer would be the first up and the last to go to bed in his household. He would not be always gadding off to towns, wasting his time in taverns and ale-houses where he would very likely get into quarrels. Absolute necessity was the only good reason for going to markets and fairs. Such jaunts were much too likely to prevent a farmer from attending to his proper affairs at home. They led to stupid bargains made under the optimistic influence of drink.

1. Ploughing in Henry VIII's reign. From Fitzherbert, *Boke of Husbandrye*, 1523

2. (*top*): GRAFTING FRUIT TREES. From Leonard Mascall. *The Countryman's New Art of Planting*, 1652. (1st. ed. 1572)
3. (*bottom*): HOP-PICKING. "The best and readyest way to take the hoppes from the poales." From Reynold Scot, *A Perfite Platform of a Hoppe Garden*, 1576.

4. A BERKSHIRE FARMHOUSE. Though a nineteenth-century drawing, this is probably a Tudor house. From Francis Stevens, *Views of Cottages and Farmhouses in England and Wales*, 1815

5. (*top*): "The Industrious Chymick bee." Bee-keeping was very essential in the days before sugar was freely imported. This is a late Tudor or early Stuart drawing.

6. (*bottom*): THRESHING WITH THE FLAIL. From Crescentius, *De Omnibus Agriculturae Partibus*, 1548

7. A CHESHIRE DAIRY FARM IN 1815—in good repair, probably
built in Tudor times. From Francis Stevens, 1815

8. THE SUBSTANTIAL STONE HOUSES of the northern counties do not easily decay. A Cumberland specimen in 1815. Most likely over three hundred years old. From Francis Stevens, 1815

9. PLOUGH MONDAY. The dance of Bessy and the Clown. An early nineteenth-century reconstruction

10. MAY DAY GAMES IN ELIZABETHAN TIMES. From an old engraving

11. Ploughing, broadcasting and harrowing, 1635. From Orwin, *The Open Fields*, 1938. (This, and Plates Nos. 12 and 13 were photographed from drawings made by Miss Helena Orwin, faithfully copied from the Laxton map of 1635. By permission of Dr. C. S. Orwin)

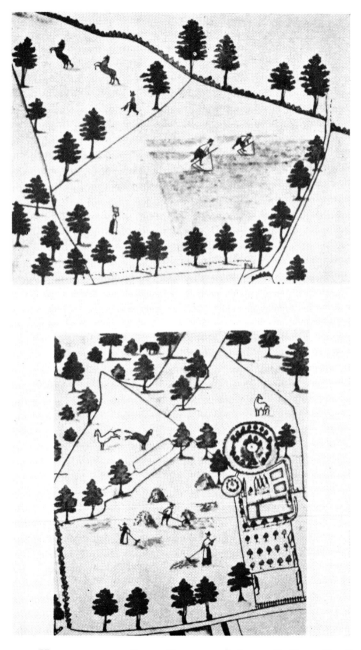

12. HAYMAKING, 1635. By permission of Dr. C. S. Orwin from *The Open Fields*, 1938

13. HARVESTING, 1635. By permission of Dr. C. S. Orwin from *The Open Fields*, 1938

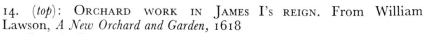

14. (*top*): ORCHARD WORK IN JAMES I'S REIGN. From William Lawson, *A New Orchard and Garden*, 1618

15. (*bottom*): BROADCASTING SEED AND HARROWING WITH OXEN. Though taken from a mid-nineteenth-century engraving this is, except for the top-hats, a good picture of how the work was done two hundred years before, and even earlier

16. THE SPREAD OF COMMERCIAL FARMING made the surveying of property important. Surveyors at work. From John Norden, *A Surveyor's Dialogue*, 1607

17. CARTING IN A TWO-WHEELED CART, on pack-saddles, and other uses and treatment of horses. From *The English Farrier*, 1636

18. A late Elizabethan or early Stuart bridal procession.
From an early nineteenth-century engraving

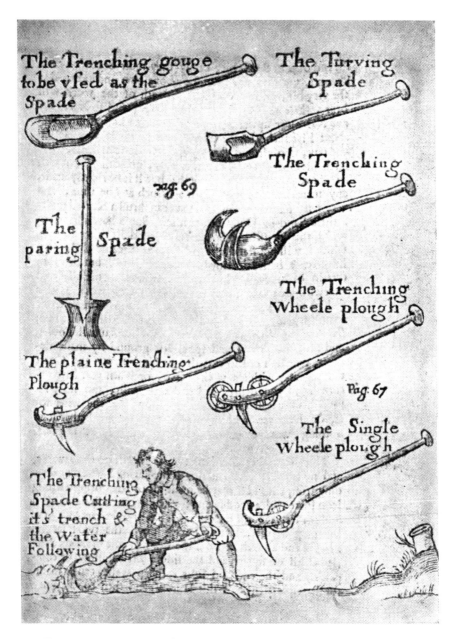

The Trenching gouge to be vfed as the Spade

The Turving Spade

The Trenching Spade

pag. 69

The paring Spade

The Trenching Wheele plough

The plaine Trenching Plough

Pag. 67

The Single Wheele plough

The Trenching Spade Cutting it's trench & the Water Following

19. DRAINING TOOLS, and a man using one of them. From Walter Blith's *The English Improver Improved*, 1653

Not only must the farmer stay at home as closely as possible, but he must make himself master of the tools and implements used about the farm. These were few and simple. The plough was the most complicated, but a good farmer ought to be able to set it for himself, and see that it was properly repaired. The actual making of the irons, share and coulter, could only be done in the blacksmith's forge, but a wise man would oversee the work carefully, and have it done to his taste. The harrow was a simple affair, a wooden frame of fairly heavy squared timber into which ashen teeth were fitted. Some of the most advanced farmers insisted on iron teeth, but nearly all used a bush harrow made of a thorn bush weighted down with a log for brushing in the seed. If the farmer had a roller it was a log of wood weighted with stones, or a cylinder of stone. Hand tools were sharpened, fitted with handles and generally kept in good order in a spare hour in the evening, but the farmer himself ought to know how to do these jobs. If he did he could tell whether they had been properly done.

The clothes named in so many farmer's inventories were considered ideal. They were worn "rather for profit than for pleasure, for which purpose shall serve garments and sleeves made of skins, caps, clothes with hoods or cassockes of canuaffe. For by this meanes there shall be no day so boysterous and cruell, wherein they (the farmer and his family) may not worke abroad." Serviceable clothes that were a protection from the weather and would not be damaged in the course of the day's work were what the farmer needed. It was not his part to go in for display.

Simple as was his clothing the Elizabethan farmer lived in a substantial house. The size and material of which it was built varied in different parts of the country, and, of course, it lacked everything that comes under the head of modern conveniences.

In Cumberland the farmer's dwelling was built of wood or clay or of rough unhewn stone if the site was convenient to a quarry. There were two rooms on the ground floor, a living-room with a wide hearth for burning peat and logs, and a bedroom for the farmer and his wife. The servants and children slept in a garret or loft above. It was reached by a ladder and was unceilinged, the roof being open to the rafters and thatch. A lean-to on the north side was used as a dairy.

The clay lump and timber farmhouses of East Anglia, many of which are still occupied, were more generous in their accommodation. A large kitchen, often used as a dining-room, and three other large rooms on the ground floor with four or five bedrooms above is not unusual. Houses of this size are scattered all over the area.

On the opposite side of the country were the granite farmhouses of the Cotswolds. The general plan was a quadrangle formed on three sides by stabling, barns, and so on. The fourth or north side was the house, all its windows looking over the courtyard. There was a kitchen, the hall and a parlour on the ground floor with bedrooms above. Many of these ancient dwellings have withstood the ravages of time and are still occupied.

Water was obtained from a well, or in less favoured districts an open pond. There was no pretence at sanitation although Sir John Harrington had invented a water-closet, and Queen Elizabeth had one installed at Richmond. It was a novelty and a toy rather than a practical thing, and was probably not to be found in half a dozen dwellings in the whole country. Lighting was restricted to tallow dips, or, luxuriously, wax tapers and candles. Heating was by open fires usually of logs or brushwood. Comfort must have been little indulged in those hardy times.

The poor husbandman and the labourer were in less happy case. His hours of labour were as long as those of the yeoman farmer. There were restrictions upon his liberty of movement. Often they were evaded, but he was continually subject to a general and meticulous surveillance. Nevertheless he was not wholly dependent upon wages, and almost every labourer was a farmer upon a small scale. Theoretically he grew his family supply of barley and maslin (a mixed crop of wheat and rye) upon the four acres of land which was the statutory minimum acreage required to be attached to each cottage. Often he had rights on the common waste for his cattle, if any, and a small enclosed garth or croft behind his cottage for any young stock he owned. With the rest of the village livestock his could be tethered on the balks in the spring, or turned out on the stubbles in the autumn. When his stock increased, if they ever did, he could rent or buy cow gates or calf gates from a neighbour. In some places he received part of his wages in kind, a practice that survived until the nineteenth century in Northumberland and other northern counties. A shepherd was often allowed to pasture some sheep on his master's land, or was given a percentage of the increase in a favourable year. The neatherd had pasture for a cow, and the husbandman a measure of grain and land on which to sow it. This custom led to the provision of a strip of potato ground, cultivated and sown for the worker, in some of the south-western counties 200 years later.

The idea that each cottage invariably had the statutory four acres attached to it has been too much emphasized. Although presentments for erecting cottages without providing the requisite acreage can be found, and although policy demanded that each man should be able to maintain himself and his family, the provisions of the statute were often evaded. In reality the labourer who occupied four acres of land was the exception rather than the rule. Indeed it is questionable whether his arduous day would have left him leisure or physical ability to work this land, and his wife and children could hardly have been wholly responsible for it.

Rural society was primitive in the extreme, and living conditions were rough and ready, as well as being self-centred owing to isolation and difficulties of communication. In these circumstances the system of farming employed could be little other than traditional. A partisan writer has said that the progress of farming technique came to a halt when the monasteries were dissolved because the monks were in the van. Only in the seventeenth century was there a new stirring because printed books had begun to circulate. This can hardly be true. There were several excellent printed books in the sixteenth century, including Fitzherbert, Tusser, Googe, and Mascall.

All the cereals and some of the legumes were grown on the arable. Wheat, barley, rye, oats, peas, beans, and vetches were commonplace. An occasional crop of buckwheat was grown. There were different varieties of wheat, red or white rivet for light land, red or white pollard for heavy. It was sown on a seed bed made by three ploughings, and broadcast by hand in the autumn. The ideal was to finish sowing by the end of October. Rye was also an autumn-sown crop, and was far more usual in the countryman's diet than wheat. Barley and oats were sown in the spring. The crops of beans, peas and vetches that were also sown in spring must have played some part in restoring fertility to a soil that was only manured with the scanty and innutritious dung of poor stall-fed beasts. The sheep fold was a help in this respect. The dye crops, madder, saffron, and woad were grown in some places. Hemp and flax were cultivated in tiny patches almost everywhere. Vegetable and herb gardens were cultivated in the great house grounds as well as those of the farmhouses.

Of cattle there were numerous local breeds, some of great repute for draught. Sheep, which varied widely, were milked to add to the supply of human food to the detriment of their lambs. Horses were bred almost everywhere.

The farmer's work growing the crops and tending the animals through the year was described by Thomas Tusser in mnemonic but pedestrian verse. He has been often quoted, but must be once again here. The routine of his farming year, based upon experience in East Anglia, is not unlike that of William Carnsaw of Bokelly, near Rowton on the Moor. Two such examples so widely separated in distance indicate that with minor differences this was the routine of the Tudor arable farming year.

The Cornishman made a round of visits in September, and began to sow wheat in October. Tusser supposed his farmer to have entered a farm at Michaelmas. If he meant to thrive he must pay attention to outdoors rather than indoor conveniences. Consult your interest before your fancy was his salutary advice.

Sow timely thy white wheat; sow rye in the dust; but these two grains should not be sown together. They could be mixed before being sent to the miller, if a mixed loaf was wanted. The land had been prepared for these winter crops by three ploughings during the fallow year and the ox teams had turned in the barley or spring crop stubble in the previous autumn. The twy-fallow had been done in the spring and the thry-fallow or third ploughing in the summer. By this means some of the weeds were destroyed, but Shakespeare commented upon the prevalence of weeds in arable crowded with "rank fumitor and furrow weed, with burdocks, hemlock, nettles, cuckoo flower". Tusser thought that beans could be lightly scattered in, but that wheat, rye and peas should not be sown too thin. Barley and dredge corn should be broadcast with a plentiful hand. These differences in seeding called for great skill on the part of the sower, who had to judge the rate by the speed with which his hand emptied the seed tip.

As soon as the autumn corn was sown, then mother and boy must be out with some kind of alarum to scare the crows, pigeons and rooks. If they were armed with slings for stones or a bow and quiver of arrows to kill off some of these pests so much the better. Water furrows, too, must be cleared at once so that no stagnant water could lie on the land during the winter.

It was unwise to be in too great a hurry to gather apples and other fruit. Apples must not be gathered before Michaelmas or they would not keep. The lazy man could beat or shake them off the tree. He was justly rewarded. Fruit harvested in this indolent way "with bruising in falling, soon faulty will be". Stable and cowhouse repairs that had slipped out of mind during the warm and busy days of summer could no longer be neglected. All must be made tight and tidy against the wet and winds of winter. Hops, if grown, must be picked. This comparatively new crop was then cultivated much more generally than it is today. Besides Kent and Worcester, it was to be seen in Essex, Yorkshire and Cornwall. Probably hops were grown elsewhere, too.

The livestock that had been wandering on the waste during the summer required some attention in the autumn. Rams and young bulls must be gelded. The boar must be cared for in his pen, and Cisley, the good dairy wench, had to "make cleanly his cabin, for measling and stench". Foresight commanded that brushwood and timber for fuel and repairs should be fetched home; so must bracken for bedding in cowshed and stable. All too soon the ways would be miry and practically impassable till spring came round again.

Out of doors in October the barley ground had to be ploughed and layed up dry and round. The thresher worked in the barn preparing seed wheat that was carefully hand-picked by "maids, little and great". The best seed was sown first upon the pea edich (stubble); the poorer seed was only used last as a dire necessity. The best rotation was barley, peas, wheat, fallow. A note to be remembered was "Who soweth in rain, he shall reap it with tears". Middlesex men who intended to sow wheat after barley put on a heavy dressing of compost and ploughed it in.

For health's sake any animal that died ought to be buried at once, but "measled" pigs could either be shut up to heal "Or kill it for bacon, or souse it to sell, For Flemming that loves it so daintily well". This piece of advice needs no comment. A good thing to do in October was to gather sloes and keep them in straw for use if either the cows or the farmer and his wife should suffer from "flix" (dysentery).

November work was done mainly indoors. Beasts were killed occasionally from then till Lent. Their fresh offal was best for the household, but most of the beasts destined for slaughter had to die then to conserve feed. Beef and bacon, even mutton, was hung in the chimney to dry in the smoke of the wood fire. Pork was pickled, brawned and soused. The thresher was busy all the winter providing grain for bread and beer and fresh straw for such livestock as it was possible to keep alive. Green peas were sown at Hallowtide, but grey peas or "runcivals" were not sown till Candlemas in February. Garlick and beans, for use before the peas were ready, ought to be sown on St. Edmund's Day (20th November) when the moon was on the wane. A careless and irascible worker was often inclined to beat the animals with his plough staff and whip stock. A careful master would very soon put a stop to such bad behaviour, and would be on the watch against other bad habits such as pilfering grain from the threshing floor. If a man carried a great leather bottle of drink to work with him, he could easily fill it with barley or wheat and carry it home. Watchfulness would soon discourage such knavish tricks.

Manure was always scarce on Tudor farms, and wise farmers adopted various expedients to increase the supply. In Essex and no doubt in other counties the headlands were ploughed up or dug up with the spade, to rot during the winter into compost. The "foul privies" of the household were cleansed and their contents buried in trenches in the garden "to make many things better to grow". A compost heap was made in the yard, and the horse-keeper was exhorted not to forget it. This was reasonable because the horses were stabled when the ploughing was finished.

December was not a month when much could be done in the fields except ditching and hedging, but if the weather was too bad for this work, a man could keep himself warm by splitting logs for firewood. There were a good many other odd jobs that could be overtaken at this dead season of the year. Tools that required sharpening could be attended to and things that had been left out of doors by hurried or careless users could be collected. If any repairs to handles or shafts were necessary, the winter was the time to make them. The cattle, housed for the winter, were carefully tended, fed as well as possible and kept comfortable and dry with fresh, clean bedding. The compost heap was added to from time to time. If new trees were necessary to replace old worn-out stock in the orchard, they should be planted before Christmas, a rule that was neglected by William Carnshaw. He planted pear trees on 31st December.

But the great thing in December was Christmas. For a fortnight the Lord of Misrule played his pranks and everyone joined in a series of frolics and feasting. The hall was thronged with the family, the servants, the tenants of the manor great and small. Then the great yule-log, dragged home through the snow, blazed and smoked on the hearth, gigantic meals were cooked and eaten, and even more gigantic feats of drinking were performed. Dancing and song resounded to the music of the minstrels in the gallery. All was gaiety and enjoyment with,

> "Good bread and good drink, a good fire in the hall,
> Brawn, pudding and souse, and good mustard withall.
>
> Beef, mutton and pork, shred pies of the best,
> Pig, veal, goose and capon, and turkey well dres't
> Cheese, apples and nuts, jolly carols to hear
> As them in the country is counted good cheer."

But all good things must end. After the last ploy of Plough Monday, it was necessary to bid feasting adieu. Once more work in the fields began with a fallow ploughing of the peas ground, provided the weather allowed. Hedging and ditching and adding to the compost heap were other jobs that were taken up again in January. If the ground was not too hard or too wet, some work could be done in the garden, orchard and coppice.

Another thing that a far-seeing farmer could do in January was to pay some attention to his pasture. If sticks and stones were gathered and any holes filled up, the mower would have an easier job when the hay was fit to cut. He would not blunt the edge of his scythe on humps in the ground, nor rick it on a stone.

After Christmas feed for the livestock began to get scarce. Many cattle were so poorly fed that they waxed faint and looked poorly and thin. Only when the new spring of grass came in with May would they fully recover from their winter short commons, and then the cowherd and his master had to take great care to ensure that they did not bloat themselves. A temporary remedy for winter faintness in cattle was to

> "Take verjuice and heat it, a pint for a cow,
> Bay salt, a handful, to rub tongue ye wot how;
> That done, with the salt, let her drink of the rest;
> This many times raiseth the feeble up beast."

Lambs were born and the shepherd worked long hours. He noted the ewes that gave birth to twins, and saved their lambs to breed from. Early calves were housed and suckled for the first fifty days of their life. Then they were weaned.

Preparation for spring sowing began. Oats were sown but for barley it was wise to give two ploughings at least before seed time in March. A man went before the plough with a mattock to stub out bushes and cumbersome roots—a striking commentary on the state of the plough-land.

All this work continued and intensified in February. The barley land was dunged from the compost heap and peas were sown. A boy leading a harrow followed the plough and covered the seed. The mole-hills that had been covered during the winter to add to the compost heap were spread about the pasture and the mole catcher engaged to trap these creatures. The plough oxen were given a modicum of hay that had been carefully saved for them. The cows got straw, or whatever else could be found. It was no wonder they gave little; the wonder was that they gave any milk. The Tudor farmer's most serious problem grew more serious as the winter went on. This was the shortage of winter feed that pressed so heavily upon his limited resources and limited the progress of his technique.

By March the year's work was getting into its stride and the arable fields were full of busy people. They sowed more peas, they sowed barley and they set hops. Immediately the seed was sown, a boy harrowed it in, and he carried a sling to drive off or destroy the crows.

Then as soon as the barley showed after a dew, the crops were rolled. The roller served two purposes. It consolidated the seed bed and made the land level for the convenience of the mowers at harvest time. At about the same time the roller was taken over any wheat land "where the clods be great". The industrious gardener began to sow vegetables for the summer in his carefully prepared tilth. Tusser recommended no less than forty-two seeds and herbs for the kitchen, twenty-two herbs and roots for salads and sauces, eleven for boiling and buttering, seventeen herbs for the still, and twenty-five for the physic garden, with others for strewing (on floors) and for windows and pots. Gardeners, usually the wife and children, must perforce be up and doing. Fruit trees were grafted in March, too.

Dog worrying of sheep is perennial, and was a curse to the Tudor shepherds. Great mastiffs were kept for house protection and thousands of mongrel curs roamed at large. The rambles of these destructive animals was a shocking worry, but was compensated by the better weather of April, and by the Easter festivity in church and home. Barley sowing, if any had not been done, must be completed in April. For the rest in early country the livestock could be turned out on the commons. Carnsaw sent his cattle to the moor in April; in later districts "cow-meat" was still wanting. This month the careful husbandman filled and stacked stores of timber for all his purposes, elm and ash for carts and ploughs, hazel for forks, sallow for rakes, and thorn for flails. Mistress and maid too, were busy in the dairy, where butter and cheese making began once again and continued "till Andrew be past" (30th November).

Some farmers did their second ploughing, or twy-fallowing for wheat in April, but in Cambridge and Lincolnshire they made their fallow in May, arguing that this late ploughing forced the weeds and was worth any two ploughings at other times of the year.

Carnsaw spent some time in May rooting and trimming the meadow; Tusser would have thought this rather late. On the other hand he sheared and sorted his sheep in that month; Tusser would have thought that early. The East Anglian farmer parted the lambs from the ewes and saved some ewes for milking to add to the resources of the dairy. Five ewes were estimated to yield as much milk as one cow; but it was very easy to overdo milking ewes. Tusser warned his readers not to be too bold about it. Where the wheat was too rank the flock was turned into it to fill their hungry bellies and keep the growth down. Now the weeds began to grow as fast as the grain, and the whole family turned out to root them out. There was still some sowing to do, too, in May. Brank (buckwheat), peas, and hemp and flax must all be finished during the month. The thresher too must finish off his work in the barn so that it would be empty before the harvest was ready to come in. Compost was carried out and spread. The farmer who came home from the fields without carrying a stone or two off was stupid, although women and children were employed on picking stones as they were on weeding. The calves were turned out to grass, and it was important to see that they had access to a good supply of drinking water.

Essex farmers caught up with Cornwall in June, when they washed and sheared the sheep and doubtless feasted joyfully after it was done.

If the hay was ready it was mown, though not till after the twy-fallow was finished. If the weather was very good a man could plough till ten o'clock. After that hour he could get on with hay carting. It is not clear when he slept during the harvest. Once again the carts and other needful things for this work and the corn harvest were overlooked. Anything lacking was provided, and damage or wear repaired. Shrubs, brambles and brakes were cut. Many ditches and ponds dry up in the summer and the mud from the bottom of these make good compost. Digging it out made them more serviceable in the winter, so this work was a two-fold gain.

Hay harvest was finished in July. Every headland was mown. The rough grass there was only thin and poor, but would serve a turn when the time came. Every little helped in these days of scanty winter feed, before any seeds, hay or roots were cultivated. Thry-fallowing or the third ploughing was done in July; only an indolent farmer would neglect it. The farmer's wife was as busy as her husband. She and her maidens gathered hemp seeds and pulled flax.

> "While wormwood had seed, get a handfull or twain;
> To save against March, to make flax to refrain;
> Where chamber is sweeped, and wormwood is strown,
> No flea, for his life, dare abide to be known."

The thry-fallow finished and the compost spread the peak of the year's work came in July and August when corn harvest began.

The wheat, rye and oats were reaped, the barley mown, maids reaped the mustard seed, and the peas and beans were got home. All these labours meant long hours and many workers in those days of manual toil; and the year's work only ended to begin again at once. Meanwhile there was rejoicing.

> "Come home, lord, singing,
> Come home, come bringing
> 'Tis merry in hall
> Where beards wag all."

Bringing home the last load of corn was a joyous affair. A foreign visitor, Paul Hentzner, saw it once when he was returning to his inn at Windsor. He and his friends "happened to meet some country people *celebrating their harvest home*; their last load of corn they crown with flowers, having besides an image richly dressed, by which perhaps they would signify Ceres, this they keep moving about, while men and women, men and maid servants, riding through the streets in the cart, shout as loud as they can till they arrive at the barn. The farmers here do not bind up their corn in sheaves . . . but directly they have reaped or mowed it put it into carts and convey it to their barns."

This last must have been peculiar to Berkshire. In other places the corn was certainly bound into sheaves. After the last sheaf was stacked or stored, a festive meal of unwonted luxury was provided by the master. It was accompanied by copious drinking, and the singing of traditional songs.

After this pleasant interlude the farmer had to attend to one of the things that annoyed him then and continued to annoy him until just before World War II. It was the payment of his tithe. Tusser exhorted the farmer always to be prompt in making this payment, perhaps to enable him to keep his irritation within bounds, perhaps so that some small item not handed over at the time might not give rise to a dispute with the parson.

Practically every kind of farm produce was taxed in this way, but in some places, as at Finmere in Oxfordshire, part of the payment had been commuted. No tithe of hay was paid in that parish, the rector having as compensation a piece of the village mead called Tithe Meadow and an enclosure of pasture named Parson's Holms. A money payment of 2s. 8d. was made for the Park and the same for the mill. The warren paid 2s. 4d. annually.

A terrier of the Glebe dated 29th October, 1601, records that

"All other places in the field doth pay the corne and the hay; tythe lambs is paid the third day of May, and the tenth night and the tenth morning we have tythe milk, and so every 10 night and 10 morning until Martinmas day in the morning (11th November), the tythe of a calfe if killed is the shoulder, if it be sold the tenth penny, if it be weaned a halfpenny; the offering is a penny a piece at Easter (and everybody had to go to church under pain of a fine); we have tythe eggs on Good Friday and at Easter every garden a penny; tythe wool when they sheare; a morticary when they dye; at christening cresam; tythes hemp; tythes piggs; tythes of bees; tythe fruit and apples and peares, etc."

Collecting his tithe must have kept the parson busy, and he must have found it difficult to trace defaulters, while the farmer who had exceptionally good crops must have felt injured because he had to part with more of them without being paid. The parishioners were compensated to some extent by obligations upon the clergy that varied from place to place. One rector had to provide bread, cheese and beer for all his congregation after afternoon service on Christmas Day, and a dinner to all householders and wives within the following twelve days, a custom that fell into disuse during the troubled times of the Commonwealth.

Throughout the sixteenth century there was a slowly increasing commercialism developing in rural life. The most marked example was the trade in wool that caused some of the enclosures, but there was trade in corn and meat as well. Nevertheless and particularly in the parts of the country more remote from London both the country gentleman and the farmer lived very largely upon the produce of their own land. As always there must have been a good deal of exchange of goods between neighbours. Many records of presents of game, cakes, homemade wine and so on, are to be found in diaries and notebooks of the time. The system of farming and the knowledge of the day only enabled the farmers to secure small and fluctuating yields of grain and to keep few and small livestock. Food enough there was in the ordinary way, but when a bad year came along famine faced the village community. It is significant, as Mr. A. L. Rowse has pointed out, that legislation against enclosure was coincident with periods of dearth, like the more serious troubles of the following century.

Home industry provided most of the necessities of life, and the countryside was searched for wild fruit and herbs for food and medicine as well as for nettles for fibre. Leather from the hides of cow, sheep and pig provided breeches, and bottles for the drink that was poured into cups made of cow horns. Textiles were made from the home-grown hemp and flax. Straw collars for the horses and wooden yokes for the oxen were produced by their ingenious users. Harness was made of rope. Most things that were included in the simple necessities of the time could be made at home. Some of the tasks were light and agreeable, but in combination they were continuous. Life in a Tudor village for everybody was rough and ready, lacking in the conveniences we have come to regard as necessities. It was the only life they knew, and consequently tolerable, often hilariously enjoyable, frequently miserably poor, always fluctuating between plenty and poverty as the seasons ran, but it had many elements the modern town dweller considers most desirable, and which the poets of the time did not fail to appreciate.

CHAPTER TWO

The Early Stuart Farmer, 1603–1660: under James I, Charles I and the Commonwealth

THE EARLY YEARS of the seventeenth century were a time of great promise. The new landowners, some of the gentry and some of the wealthier yeomen, were everywhere looking to new methods and improved breeding to increase their income and profits. All over the country waste uncultivated land was slowly being reclaimed and made into farms. The Peak of Derbyshire was being settled; so were the wastes of Lancashire, round Rossendale and elsewhere. In similar country in the west and south-west there was the same activity. The men of Devon were considered to be in the forefront of advanced farming. Suffolk and Essex farmers at the other side of the country were their close competitors. In the eastern counties the drainage of the Fens was being planned and attempted, though not as yet with much success. The farming textbooks of the day recommended new crops and new manures. Optimistic inventors protected new ideas for implements by Letters Patent. They probably did not make their ideas concrete either in small scale models or in large.

But there were many misfortunes. Severe outbreaks of plague occurred in 1603 and 1625, and there were severe and prolonged dearths. At the end of Queen Elizabeth's reign there were three years of bad harvests in 1595, 1596 and 1597. There was famine in 1608 and 1630, and great scarcity in the 1620s. From 1646 to 1650 there were poor

42

harvests and continuous scarcity of food. In these famine years prices were naturally high, and the farmer who held what he had for a rise was heartily condemned in contemporary literature. Ben Jonson's command of invective called him,

"a precious, dirty damned rogue
That fats himself with expectation
Of rotten weather . . ."

one who told himself

"O, I shall make my prices as I list;
What though a world of wretches starve the while?
He that will thrive, must think no course vile!"

Already there was an opposition of interest between the court and the country that is so frequently discussed in prose and poem, in pamphlet and broadside. It is indeed not impossible that one underlying cause of the final outbreak of the Civil War was the hunger of people faced with the sight of some few getting rich when the majority were short of food.

Government was unsettled during all but the very first years of this period. Quarrels and bickerings in the reign of James I culminated in Civil War under Charles I. It is difficult to assess the extent to which the ordinary routine of village life was affected by the wars. At Darrington in Yorkshire affairs "went on very much as usual, men planting and sowing, reaping and garnering in the accustomed way, while the primitive cannon flung their balls from Baghill across the valley into the grim walls built five hundred years before by the Normans under Ilbert de Lacy". There must have been hundreds of other villages all over the country that were equally placid because armed activity was sporadic and localized at different times during the campaign. Unrest there must have been, though many rustic people took no part in the fighting at all except when they tried to protect their own goods from one army or the other. But the upper classes were arrayed on either side and this must have affected the lower classes closely. Transfers of property, especially during the wars and the Commonwealth, and afterwards at the Restoration, must at least have caused uncertainty of tenure and uneasiness amongst the farming community. Together the plagues, the famine years, and the civil disturbances of the first half of the seventeenth century were disastrous. This combination of circumstances made null and void much of the brilliant promise of the early years of the century.

Nevertheless many men led pleasant, and even profitable lives. The squire's day in James I's reign was peaceful and enjoyable enough. One of them, a squire and farmer, too, Barnaby Googe, gentleman, of Lincolnshire, has recorded that in summer he was often first of all to rise in the morning. In winter he was not so energetic and might leave things to his steward if he did not feel inclined to get up. His wife could leave the household work to her maid if she chose. When he had time, doubtless a euphemism for inclination, and in pleasant weather, he oversaw everything himself. He remembered the old saying that the best dung for the fields is the master's foot, and the best provender for the horse the master's eye. When he had set everyone to work he went into his study to "serve God and read the Holy Scriptures". Next he made notes of what needed doing, and did whatever business was necessary. A little before dinner he strolled in the garden, or in the field, or, if it was wet weather, in the gallery of his house. He dined about eleven o'clock, quite simply, on an egg, a chick, a piece of kid or veal, fish, butter and such like. Sometimes he had a salad or fruit that was in season, food that cost him only the growing. It pleased him as well as if he had had the daintiest dish in Europe. After dinner he chatted with his wife, his servants, his guests if there were any, and then went once more about the estate to look at the men, the fields and the stock. He read a little again when he came home, and then supped "on a small pittance". The day ended watching the sheep come home, the plough oxen dragging slowly towards the byre with weary legs, looking over the cattle, or strolling wherever fancy led him. Finally plans were made with his wife and servants of what should be done next day. Two or three hours after supper he went to bed. This was his routine several times a week if not every day. A most simple and satisfying life.

This farming squire was a sample of many such dignified, easy-going, pleasant people. Sober, industrious, rather Puritanical, though not necessarily Roundhead, they went on in the even tenor of their way. Their whole interest was their local politics, their farming and hunting, and had little or no concern with the turmoils that disturbed the Metropolis. Both the farming squire and the wealthy yeoman kept cattle and sheep. They cut the natural meadow hay and grew wheat, barley, rye, oats, beans, peas, tares and vetches and perhaps a little hemp and flax. Many grew hops, and that in districts where they are today unknown. In some places there were cherry and apple orchards, a few pear and other fruit trees in the hedgerows. Nuts were gathered in the woods. A few people planted mulberry trees, quinces and bullaces. These all, like Barnaby Googe, had a steward or bailiff, but preferred to guide and oversee most of the work for themselves.

These men's thoughts dwelt on the improvement of their farms rather than upon the dispute at Court though in the end many of them were drawn into the conflict. Like Robert Loder at Harwell, Berks, they were willing to try new things. He used his malt dust as manure. He tethered animals on his hitchings in the open arable fields, the plots of weeds and grass he had not cultivated that season. He did not hesitate one spring to plough in a crop of autumn corn that failed and to resow the land with spring corn. He often got yields as high as the modern national average, but hardly so much as the exceptional return Herrick rejoiced about in his lines:

> "Lord, 'tis thy plenty dropping hand
> That soils my land,
> And gives me for my bushel sown
> Twice ten for one."

If the poet sowed two and a half bushels an acre, a normal seeding, he got fifty bushels return and though such yields have been recorded it is very certain they were most unusual.

Sowing seed was always done by hand broadcasting and this was a job demanding great skill as well as being tedious. Already in the early seventeenth century writers were beginning to discuss other methods. Dibbling, which they called setting, was discussed by Sir Hugh Plat and Edward Maxey. Gabriel Plattes proposed a machine for sowing. The effect of these writings was not pronounced, but at least one farming squire, or rather his lady, concerned herself with setting corn on a field scale.

Lady Hoby, living on her husband's estate near Scarborough, noted in her diary that she acted as steward in her husband's absence. One

October she "walked to see some wheat; walked about to workmen, and was busied setting some wheat; was sometimes at the plowers, and had sowen of rye five pecks; was busy about setting corne!" She did many other things, but there the important act was setting corn. If this practice had been introduced upon this estate for only a small proportion of the area sown, is it too much to believe that a few other of the most advanced landowners might have tried it as well? This is not to suggest that the practice was in any sense general; only that a few farmers of the best kind, units only no doubt, were trying this novel method.

These were the more sober characters, but were typical of a large proportion of rural families, the Verneys of Buckinghamshire, the Evelyns of Surrey, the Ishams of Northampton, and innumerable others whose names and notions are known to us through family histories, diaries and the like.

Quite other was the sporting type, "the copy of our ancient nobility", exemplified in Mr. Hastings of Woodlands in Hampshire. His main preoccupation was country sports, and his home was cluttered with the apparatus of the chase. All manner of sports hounds lay about in the great hall. "His neighbours grounds and royalties were free to him, who bestowed all his time on these sports but what he borrowed to caress his neighbours wives and daughters; there being not a woman in all his walks, of the degree of a yeoman's wife and under, and under the age of forty, but it was extremely her fault if he was not intimately acquainted with her." The husbands and brothers were always welcome at Woodlands. "There he found beef, pudding, and small beer in great plenty; a house not so neatly kept as to shame him and his dirty shoes; the great hall strow'd with marrow bones, full of hawks' perches, hounds, spaniels and terriers. . . ."

A table at one end of the hall formed the office and bore a church *Bible* and *Book of Martyrs*. For the rest both table and desk were covered with hawks' hoods, bells and such like. Squire Hastings's table did not cost much. The food and drink was home produced, plentiful and wholesome. Drink was served by the glass for the Squire did not tolerate drunkenness, an odd restriction in such a man.

He was well natured but soon angry, calling his servants bastards and cuckoldy knaves, in one of which he often spoke truth to his own knowledge and sometimes in both, though of the same man. He lived to be a hundred, never lost his eyesight, but always wrote and read without spectacles and got on horseback without help. Until fourscore he rode to the death of the stag as well as any.

Men like Hastings appeared uncouth at Court or in London, and were bitterly lampooned by some contemporaries. They were great men in the village and among their tenants, but were shy and timid in the company of their equals. Yet they were Justices of the Peace and largely responsible for ensuring the decrees of government were carried out in their locality. They discussed statutes and husbandry well enough to make their neighbours think them wise men, and were skilled in arithmetic and rates, so careful in expense that when they travelled they would go ten miles out of the way to a cousin's house to save expense. In that day of generous vails they would reward the cousin's servants by shaking their hands when they departed. Something must be deducted from this description, but the smaller squires were doubtless comfortable and at their ease in their normal surroundings, a little uncertain of themselves in the strange conditions of London if they ever visited the place, and economical in expense as their incomes forced them to be. They were however growing richer like many of the yeomen who so much resembled them, and aped them.

In Middlesex there were not a few yeomen "who wade in the weedes of gentlemen". They only supervised their farms, and organized the work of their employees, seldom or never setting their own hand to the plough. These were the grasiers who had great feedings for cattle and good stock for breeding. They sold their fat beasts at Smithfield, and bought stores there and at other markets turning a pretty penny in the process. In Essex, Hertfordshire and elsewhere such men thrived and reaped a common satire with the squirearchy in the "characters" that were then so popular a form of writing. They were formally religious, but hated paying tithe, the value of which they would rather have spent upon their own men. They were not highly educated, and spoke the dialect of their neighbourhood. They ached to win more land for themselves and to purchase arms, the visible sign of gentry. This ambition consumed them and often resulted in the adoption of some absurd emblem like a pair of harrows or a cuckoo. With all these rather unamiable qualities they were hospitable and lived well. "The pride of his housekeeping is a mess of cream, a pig or a green goose." Again he "preserves a chandler's mess of bacon, links and pudding in the chimney corner". And he had the virtue of feeling that keeping a good table he was an honest man. He did not disdain early rising and spending the day in the fields and woods.

Widely distributed all over the country were the lesser yeomen who "wholy dedicate themselves to the manuringe of their lande. And theis commonlye are so furnished with kyne that the wyfe or twice or thrice a weeke conveyeth to London (or to some local market) mylke, butter, cheese, apples, peares, frumentye, hens, chyckens, egges, baken and a thousand other country drugges, which good housewifes can frame and find to get a pennye." All these things helped to add to what the husband made of his corn.

Besides their small farming enterprises, many of the less well-to-do yeomen engaged in subsidiary businesses. Often they kept an ale-house, probably managed by a wife or daughter, or they became the local miller, went in for some kind of retail trade by keeping one of the few shops that were to be found in the market towns, or ran a smithy either personally or by proxy, perhaps a son. When the harvests were bad these men, whose enterprises were so uneasily balanced between prosperity and poverty, infringed upon the industrial regulations of the day by "exercising trades to which they had not been apprenticed". In 1631–32, a bad year, a large number were prosecuted (as we should say) for doing just this. The trained craftsmen, who were in none too good a case that year of poor trade, resented this infringement of their legal rights and of their insecure livelihood.

The greater yeoman or the lesser squires found much more re-munerative opportunities in the clothing trade and in the slowly developing coal and iron trades, and in the nascent potteries.

The employer, be he squire or yeoman, had the choice of what he should do, provided he did what was necessary. He could, if he were so inclined, stay in bed in the morning, or, if the weather was too evil, he could stay in the house, and find some interesting or entertaining occu-pation. For the worker, be he working yeoman, poor husbandman or ploughman, there was little choice.

The demands of the beasts in his charge were continuous, and his work therefore continuous from his rising up to his lying down. The ploughman's day (and ploughman was a generic term for the three classes named) began at four o'clock in the morning. After saying his prayers he went at once to the stables to fodder his cattle and muck out the house. He rubbed down the plough oxen and curried the cart horses. He took them both to water, and then fed them again in the stable. While the animals were eating, the ploughman looked to his harness and got everything ready to begin work. All this occupied about two hours. At six o'clock he had a well-earned half hour for breakfast.

The next half hour was spent in yoking up. At seven o'clock the ploughman set off to the fields, where he worked till two or three o'clock in the afternoon. He then brought the cattle home, rubbed them down, cleaned and fed them. Next came dinner to which servants and family alike brought good appetites. At four the cattle were rubbed down again, cleaned out and given more fodder. When this was done, a supply of feed was made ready for the next day, "Whether it be hay, straw, or bed fodder", whatever was to hand. After preparing it, the ploughman carried it to the stable. While there he watered and foddered the cattle and horses again.

By this time it was getting on for six o'clock, and supper was ready. Having eaten this well-earned meal—he had already been at work with only short breaks for fourteen hours—the ploughman could sit by the fire and do odd jobs. He mended shoes for the family, crushed hemp and flax for his wife to manufacture, crushed apples and crabs for cider and verjuice, ground malt, picked rushes for candles and did a thousand and one other jobs that had to be done in a self-sufficient household.

At eight o'clock, rather wearily, he attended to the cattle again, saw that they were safely tied, mucked out again, and gave them feed for the night. The strenuous day was over when this was done, and he could go to rest, "giving God thanks for benefits received that day".

The shepherd's life was equally fully occupied, but some of his day could be spent in sitting in the shade. Always from Theocritus until quite recently the shepherd's life has been idealized as if the season were always spring or summer, and his work little more than watching the gambols of the young lambs in the sunshine. Give him fat lambs and fair weather and the shepherd knows no happiness beyond them, was an early Stuart opinion. The sweet fountain was his fairest alehouse; the sunny bank his best chamber. The nearest thicket would shelter him or his home was not too distant. His flock provided all his

D

raiment, outside and linings, cloth and leather, and instead of much costly linen his little garden yielded hemp enough to make his "lock-ram" shirts. His daily life was looked upon as delightful work, whatever it might be; whether to mend his garments, cure a diseased sheep, instruct his dog, or change pastures, all of which he did at his own choice and not under orders for he was the master of his master's flock. The worst temptation of his idleness was said to teach him no more mischief "than to love entirely some nut-brown milkmaid, or hunt the squirrel, or make his cosset wanton". This is all very nice, but it takes no note of wild work in the winter snow; living with the ewes when they were lambing in the cold early months of the year; of the long hours of sheep-dipping, tarring, and attending to feet against the rot; of the hours spent in changing fold hurdles; the dusty, often itchy, work of shearing.

Perhaps it was these disadvantages that made it difficult for some people to get a good shepherd. Leonard Mascall of Plumpton, Sussex, deplored the character of some shepherds. He had his own idea of what a shepherd ought to be, and what he was usually not. He

"ought to be of good nature, wise, skilful, countable, and right in all his doings, wherein few are to be found at this day, especially in Villages and Townes, for by their idleness and long rest they grow to waxe stubborne, and are given (for the most part) to frowardness and evil, more than good profit to their Masters, and ill mannered whereof breeds many a thievish condition, being pickers, lyars, and stealers, and runners about from place to place, with many other infinite evils."

Shakespeare knew the differences in the shepherd's life only too well. In summer it was a pretty story:

> "When shepherds pipe on oaten straws,
> And merry larks are ploughman's clocks,
> *　　　　　*　　　　　*
> And maidens bleach their summer smocks."

But it was very different in winter:

"When icicles hang by the wall,
And Dick the shepherd blows his nail,
And Tom bears logs into the hall,
And milk comes frozen home in pail,
When blood is nipped and ways be foul. . . ."

Everyone has to put up with changes in the seasons and the vagaries of the weather, but that does not make the winter or a bad summer any the more pleasant for outdoor work. No one, however hardy and inured, could have sustained life if it were all unceasing labour for sixteen or more hours a day, broken up only by a couple of short rests for meals, and eased by an alternation of light and heavy tasks usually done pretty much at the worker's own speed. The rural cycle of work was broken up by a good many religious and lay festivities, and these served to make life bearable. Holy days and the village feast of the patron saint of the parish church, brideales, christenings and funerals were all anticipated with joy (or sorrow), enjoyed with abandon, and talked over afterwards so intensely so to make rural England of that time, before the Puritans damped it down, a truly Merrie England. Since pleasures are so vividly remembered it is not surprising that poets found the country round worthy of celebration. Hedonistic old Parson Herrick did not fail to make it sound a halcyon life in lines that cannot be too often quoted from his *Idyllica*:

"For sports, for pageantry and plays,
Thou hast thine eves and holy days;
On which the young men and maids meet,
To exercise their dancing feet.
Tripping the comely country round
With daffodils and daisies crown'd.
Thy wakes, thy quintals, here thou hast
Thy maypoles too with garlands graced;
Thy morrice dance; thy Whitson ale;
The shearing feasts that never fail;
Thy harvest home; thy wassail bowl,
That's tossed after Fox i' the hole;
Thy mummeries; thy Twelve-tide kings,
And queens; the Christmas revellings,

Thy nut brown mirth, thy russet wit,
And no man pays too dear for it.
To these thou hast thy times to go
And trace the hare i' the treacherous snow;
Thy withy wiles to draw and get
The lark into the trammel net;
Thou has thy cock-rood and thy glade
To take the precious pheasants made;
Thy lime twigs, snares and pit falls them,
To catch the pilfering birds not men."

Herrick probably wrote these lines in Devonshire, but what he said was descriptive of rustic life all over the country, then almost unbelievably sparsely populated and having wide areas of unreclaimed land. At the other end of the kingdom, the Shuttleworths were building Gawthorp Hall in Lancashire between 1600 and 1604. The site was on the edge of great deer forests well stocked with red deer. The Ribble, the Calder and Hodder abounded in salmon and trout. The otter was hunted in their valley. The moors were full of game and the cultivated lands of partridges and hares. Most of these were, of course, nominally out of the reach of Jack and his master, but they would have been much more stupid than they were if some did not come their way. The valleys were doubtless as full of skilful poachers then as well as legitimate sportsmen.

Russet wit took all sorts of forms, many of them still familiar. One was solemn chaffing of the stranger, who tried to take a rise out of the yokel. Henry Peacham was once riding near Horncastle, Lincolnshire, when he met a swineherd tending his pigs on the summer fallow field.

"My friend," he said, "you keep here a company of unruly cattle."

"Aye," quoth the swineherd, "poor souls they are indeed."

"I believe," said Peacham, "they have a language among themselves and can understand one another as well as you and I. Were they ever taught?"

"Alas, poor things, they have not a letter of the booke. I teach them all I have."

"Why what says the great hog with red spots that lies under another in his grunting language?"

"Marry he bids him lie further off."

After this lesson in pig's tongue Peacham rode on.

This is characteristic. Other witicisms were embodied in rhymes about neighbouring villages or quaint stories about people's doings. In Fressingfield, our own village, there is a story that the silly men of one nearby built a hedge to keep the cuckoo in. Market Harborough had no town field, and a local saying gibed that a goose could eat all that grows in Harborough field, that every crow that flew over it turned white. Parents threatened naughty children that they would throw them into the Harborough field.

Rhymes are innumerable. One or two are:

> "Sutton for mutton
> Carshalton for beeves,
> Epsom for whores
> And Ewel for thieves."

Many places in different counties were celebrated for pretty girls and good ale. Some rhymes related to weather lore.

> "When Breden Hill puts on his hat
> Ye men in the vale beware of that."

The schoolchildren of almost every village used to repeat doggerel of this kind until within living memory.

There was a good deal of mental activity as well as physical. The latter was exemplified in building activities like that of Shuttleworth at Gawthorpe. Gervase Markham laid down elaborate rules for a house to be built by a sufficiently well-to-do farmer, and provided a plan to work from. It was to include the great hall, a dining-parlour for the entertainment of strangers, an inward closet within the parlour for the mistress's "use for necessaries". A stranger's lodging within the parlour at the opposite end, a larder within the buttery, a spacious kitchen with room for brewing, a dairy and a milk house.

At Finmere in 1634 the Lord of the Manor occupied a house of four "bayes", sufficiently thatched and in repair. Recently he had built a barn of five "bayes", well thatched and walled. On this farm there was an old pease barn, standing upon posts, hovel-like, sufficiently in repair. Building was going on everywhere. Farmhouses and farm buildings were being extended and improved and were maintained and kept in repair by their owners and occupiers. "In most very old country houses," wrote Elizabeth Godfrey in 1903, "may still be found carpenter's bench, blacksmith's forge, and the old pots and paraphernalia of a house painter for all ordinary repairs were done at home. Besides the customary surroundings of stable, dairy, fowl house, brewery, malt house, and sometimes even a mill. There were, of course, stew ponds for fish, and where there was a large park, a decoy for wild fowl."

Tradition had a great hold upon all these people, gentleman, yeoman, poor husbandman, and labourer alike. The lower in the social scale the less likely were they to be influenced by the new ideas that industrious writers were putting about. Most of them wished to live as their fathers before them and to do their work in the same way. It was the life they had been born to, and was not something they could easily change or wished to change. There were innovators in the field like Lady Hoby or Robert Loder, but these must have been in the minority. Early Stuart writers of farming textbooks uniformly complain, as such people continued to do for centuries, that the farmers would only "shape their courses as their fathers did". They stuck to a plodding course, and would not put in practice any new device. Walter Blith said bitterly that these stubborn oafs could not be convinced even when they saw their neighbours ploughing effectively with less cattle and getting better yields. In spite of these complaints it was a time when an ingenious husbandman could break away from the traditional practice, and there is no doubt that some of them did so.

The most intensively farmed countries in Europe then were Brabant and Flanders. A good many people travelled between England and these countries. Not the least important was Sir Richard Weston of Sutton Hall, near Farnham, Surrey. From these countries the new crops were introduced that were to revolutionize English farming, and to make it world famous. Weston wrote about turnips and clover and the long rotations practised by the Dutch "boores" or peasants, and actually grew turnips on his land at Worplesdon. Some changes were being made; some progress was taking place. How much it was is difficult to estimate.

The Rev. Ralph Josselin of Earls Colne, Essex, deplored the continuous rains during the summers of 1646, 1647, and 1648 when the crops rotted in the ground or dwindled in the stack, and the fruit rotted on the trees, but he stubbornly went on with ditching and hedging. He let the job by the piece to William Webb and his brother, digging the ditches, throwing the marl into the field, cutting the hedge, setting on again, "and to go three spits were need is, to throw off a spit where I intend to quicke and to raise it up with new earth". All this was to be done for 3½d. a rod or 4d. where it was worth it.

But long after Josselin was dead old men in Buckinghamshire, who had ploughed the S-shaped ridges common in open-field husbandry, told Mr. Eland that they could only laugh at the idea that the ridges had to be made that shape because of the turning of the long teams of oxen. They maintained that the ridges were made that shape only to drain the land. "When asked why water should be expected to run better when the furrow was curved than when it was straight, one farmer of the (eighteen) 'sixties countered the question by saying, "Did you ever know a brook to run straight?" In face of that kind of argument it must have been difficult indeed to bring a change into fashion, but nevertheless it was slowly and steadily being done. Naturally the tempo increased after the ideas had been discussed for a great many years, but for the moment they remained largely, but not entirely, in the realm of theory.

The truth is, of course, that as always the farmers of some districts were more go ahead than those in others. Somerset men had made the Vale of Taunton so fertile that Norden called it the Paradise of England. Suffolk, Essex, and Surrey men grew the best hops. Farms in Kent, round Faversham and Sittingbourne, were noted for their fruit. Apple and cherry orchards cared for by Gloucestershire, Herefordshire and Worcestershire farmers were already famous. Some farmers on East Anglian light soils had grown carrots successfully. Saffron was grown by enterprising men round Saffron Walden and thence towards Cambridge. The flocks bred by Dorset sheep farmers and those in Sussex, Wilts, Hants, and Bucks, were renowned. A trial of sainfoin had been made at Cobham in Kent. Farmers in many counties were burning lime and using it as fertilizer. If they were within ten miles of the coast others collected seaweed or seasand for the same purpose. Hertfordshire men bought up London street sweepings and stable manure. The market gardeners of Tothill Fields, Chelsea, Battersea, and Fulham collected the London night soil.

Market gardens were a necessity round London, but elsewhere

nearly everyone had a piece of garden ground. A garden was part and parcel of every farm, and a fairly wide range of vegetables were grown, though some of the things in the following list were restricted to the more wealthy. All were grown if not by all. Beans, peas, cabbage, colewort and cauliflower, savoys, beet, anise, carrots, turnips, parsnips, skirrets, radishes, onions, garlic, leeks were in almost every garden; luxuries like melons, cucumbers, asparagus, artichokes, and the improved strawberry, probably in only a few.

Vegetables were not beloved of the majority. The farmers thought that the men ate more meat if their appetites were stimulated by a mess of cabbage, etc. The farm servants, who lived in, did not like to see vegetables on their platters because they believed the vegetables were used as a substitute for meat.

The main constituents of rural diet other than in the houses of the nobility and gentry were bread and white meats, cheese, butter and milk, with a little bacon to flavour the midday meal. An onion, a leek or garlic was a favourite condiment. Beef was eaten in the farmhouse when a cow was killed, or mutton when a sheep was slaughtered, but these were rare events except in the autumn. Pig meat, beef, and mutton alike were preserved by hanging in the chimney to cure in the smoke of the wood fire, or simply hung on hooks in the kitchen beams to take its chance.

Bread was made of wheat, or rye, a mixture of the two called maslin, or diluted with barley, peas, beans, lupins. At a pinch, and there were a good many pinches in this half century, acorns or beech mast were used, and nettles were boiled. Since the bread oven was brought to a heat by burning furze, brushwood or a faggot inside, and the fire only roughly scraped out before putting in the dough, this must have been polluted with wood ash on the outside. Probably that was why contemporary doctors advised their patients to cut off the crust before eating bread.

The custom of allowing the grain stubble to be gleaned by the farm workers is well known, and has often been written about. It was as much a matter of economy as of charity. Where the gleaners had been little or nothing was wasted. Every ear of corn that had been left after the sheaves had been tied was scrupulously collected. There was not enough to allow any to be wasted. The gleaners in the field, it has been said, presented a beautiful picture to the sensitive mind. Some of them were by no means as innocent as it was usual to represent them. Many were the tricks they played to ensure that there was plenty of grain to glean.

The magistrates of Dorset, for example, were constrained to interfere to try to prevent these knaves. At the Easter Session in 1635 they made an order that gleaning was a privilege only for the aged, weak, and infirm poor, only for those who had not wherewithal to maintain themselves. The constables were ordered to patrol the harvest fields with sufficient help to enable them to prevent unlawful persons gleaning. The indolent and idle must be made to go to harvest work at the regular wages upon pain of two days' imprisonment and one night in the stocks. Anyone found in the harvest fields at night was to be arrested and imprisoned until they found sureties for good behaviour.

All this was necessary because under pretence of gleaning people refused to do harvest work for wages. Others who took harvest work by the piece secretly agreed with others to glean after them, and took bribes to neglect to gather the corn together. Yet others would begin to glean before the winter corn was "mowed together", presumably in the barn, and the summer corn made into ricks. More daring characters still "walked abroad in the night" with sheets and great cloths to carry away the corn they stole. If the constables attempted to lay hands on any of these wrongdoers they were insolently threatened with an action at law.

Barnaby Googe made an odd remark about butter. It seems to imply that butter was not so generally made as cheese. The farmers, he wrote, "does chiefly commend for milke, the pasture where groweth Spery (spurrey) and Clover grasse and that is all bedeekt with yellow flowers". Butter was made from milk "though it be chiefly at this day among the Flemmings". In the *Merry Wives of Windsor*, Act II, scene ii, Shakespeare made Ford say that he would not trust a Flemming with his butter. Perhaps this means that butter was well liked in the Low Countries. Eating butter was, of course, much more ancient than the seventeenth century although not everybody believed it wholesome.

Dr. Muffett was one of these. Only the poorest people in northern Europe, including England, ate it according to his statement. There was some difficulty in keeping butter fresh, even when heavily salted. This ignorance of the art of preserving it may have been one reason why butter was not more generally used.

Cheese kept better and formed a substantial part of the farmer's and labourer's food. Making it was understood better in some counties than in others. Googe thought that "in England the best cheese is the Cheshire and the Shropshire, then the Banbury cheese, next the Suffolk and the Essex cheese and the very worst is the Kentish cheese". He quoted John Haywood.

> "I never saw Banbury cheese thicke enough
> But I have seen Essex cheese quicke enough"

and for good measure added an old saw:

> "Banbury, Langtony, Suffolke good cheese, Essex goe thou by Shropshire; cum Cheshire, Hertford may wel with the best peere."

There are some significant omissions here. Neither Cheddar, nor double Gloucester, nor Dorset blue vinney are included. If these cheeses were made then, they were eaten at home. Farmers in these places would hardly have been so unaware of their own interests as not to keep dairy cows where the natural pasture was so attractive.

Bacon was, Googe said, the chiefest supporter of the husbandman's kitchen. Norden was confounded by the herds of swine that roamed the forests of Northampton. He thought the pig "altogether unprofitable till he came to the slaughter. Then his rusty ribs on a frosty morning will please Pierce the ploughman and will so supple his weather beaten lips that his whip and his whistle will hammer out such harmony as will make a dog dance that delights it." Other counties too had great herds of swine. Hampshire was one that was noted. In Essex, too, the pigs wandered through the extensive forests. Smaller numbers were kept everywhere. The swine was prolific, and a good meat producer.

If on no other day in the week a piece of bacon was certain to grace the table for Sunday dinner unless times were unspeakably hard. And it is easy to believe the Sunday dinner in farmhouse and cottage alike was a special meal.

It deserved to be. Attendance at church was compulsory on every parishioner under pain of a fine of one shilling for each absence. Enforcement of this regulation became stricter as the Puritan feeling developed, and eminent people were not exempted. Jane Scrope, one of an ancient family, was prosecuted at the Manorial Court of Castle Coombe in 1596 for not having been at any church. In that village, a couple of years before this somewhat startling event, an order was made that all butchers should shut their shop windows before the chiming of the second bell for morning prayers. Keeping open laid them under a penalty of five shillings—some ten days' wages for a labourer in husbandry.

At Weymouth three people were fined for having been at Sandsfoot Castle one Sunday evening in 1623 and so absent from evening service. Ale-houses were closed during the hours of divine service. All over the country the constables were enjoined to seek out offending publicans and their customers. Sunday morning is still in remote villages a favourite time for the amateur barber to cut the local hair. It is often done in the dim aisles of some lofty barn. This must be a very ancient habit. It was forbidden—especially during church.

In 1610 the constables at Lyme Regis were themselves presented "for suffering unlawful games to be played . . . as well the sabbath days as the week days". Archbishop Arundel tried to put down the custom of holding fairs in churchyards on Sundays, known as keeping the wakes there.

There was an element of good in all this. The effect was to make Sunday a day when only absolutely necessary work was done. Everything else must either be completed on the day before or left until the day after. Thus was the Sabbath (Sunday, though there was some controversy about it) made a day of rest so far as possible. On the other hand there was a distinct temptation to go too far, and to say that no games, sports, or amusements might be indulged in either. The day must be one of complete rest except for church attendance. The Stuart Puritan ideal was quite equal to that of the Victorian Sunday.

Freedom to indulge in Sunday sports between church services had always, in days when the only non-alcoholic drink was water, a tendency to degenerate into license. William Jefferies petitioned the Worcestershire magistrates in 1617 to enforce stricter observance of Sunday. At Longden it was the custom to indulge in May-games, dancing and sports on Sunday. These attracted people from other places, and there was some drunkenness and quarrels. In 1614 some men from Fortington caused a riot, and one had his head broken. Next year men from Elsfield did the same. Some of the players made a nuisance of themselves in church.

The same sort of thing was happening in Lancashire. James Sturyaker and forty others "assembled at Garstang and played a drum and fife band and with branches rode and walked from a certain wood as far as Kirkeland in Garstang". This was in 1603. This and other like happenings made the Lancashire Justices issue orders in 1616 forbidding householders to keep any guest in the home during divine services. Ale-house keepers and their wives must close their premises and go to church like anyone else.

All these regulations, quite apart from whether they were right or wrong, show that the village population was determined to make the most of its leisure on the one possible day of the week. The Puritans and the deeply religious were determined to create a real Holy day out of a Sunday not very well conducted, by some, but seriously observed by a very large number of people.

A year after the Lancashire Justices had made their very strict order, James I passed through the county on his way from Scotland to England. While there he was entertained one Sunday with a sermon by the Bishop of Chester, a dinner, and about four o'clock a rush-bearing with pipers followed by supper, a masque played by the local gentry, some speeches and dancing to complete the day. The royal example provoked a petition from Lancashire people for greater freedom to spend part of Sunday in sport.

James was a reasonable man in some respects, and he desired to rule a happy and healthy people fit for labour and war. He published *The King's Book of Sports* in 1618. This set forth the excellent reasons there were for pleasant and harmless recreation on Sunday always provided that proper attendance at church was made by everybody, churchmen, Recusant, Puritans or Precisians, all alike.

The *Book* sets out the permissible sports. They were dancing for men and women, archery for men, leaping, vaulting or any such harmless recreation. May-games, Whitsun ales, Morris dances, setting up of maypoles, and other customary plays were all permissible at times that did not clash with church services. The women, too, were to be allowed to carry rushes to the church for decorating it, according to the old custom.

In all this controversy there was the beginning of the end of those

Within the illustration:

Systema
Agriculturæ.
Being
The Mystery Of Husbandry
Discovered and
layd Open
by
J W

FC Van Hove Scul.

Printed for Tho. Dring at ye Corner of Chancery lane in Fleetstreet. 1675.

20. THE FRONTISPIECE of J. Worlidge's *Systema Agriculturae*, 1669, showing a late Stuart farmhouse with the various farm work in progress

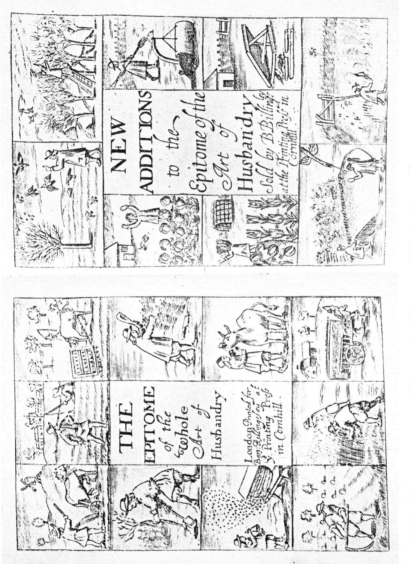

21. (*left*): FRONTISPIECE to Blagrave's *Epitome of Husbandry*, 1669
22. (*right*): FRONTISPIECE to Blagrave's *Epitome*

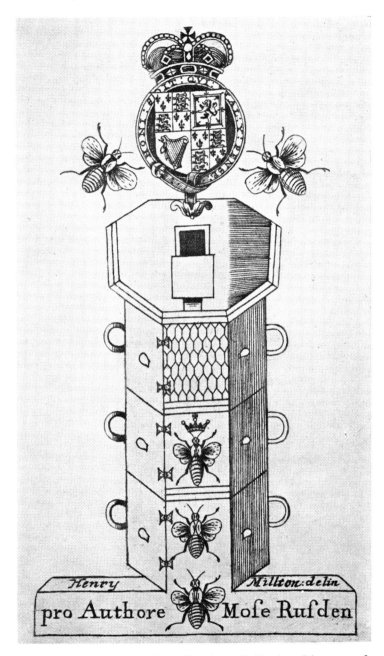

23. A BEE-HIVE from Moses Rusden. *A Further Discovery of Bees,* 1677

24. LATER STUART types of livestock. They were rather
poor. From James Lambert, *The Countryman's Treasure*,
1683

25. HARVEST WORK IN 1686. From Richard Blome's *The Gentleman's Recreation*, 1686

26. Edward Lisle, a land-owner farmer in Queen Anne's reign. Frontispiece in *Observations in Husbandry*, 2nd ed., 1757

27. JETHRO TULL, the famous inventor of the first workable seed-drill. He lived in Queen Anne's reign. From Jour. R.A.S.E., 1871.

28. The last load home at harvest. A very ancient ceremony. From an old engraving

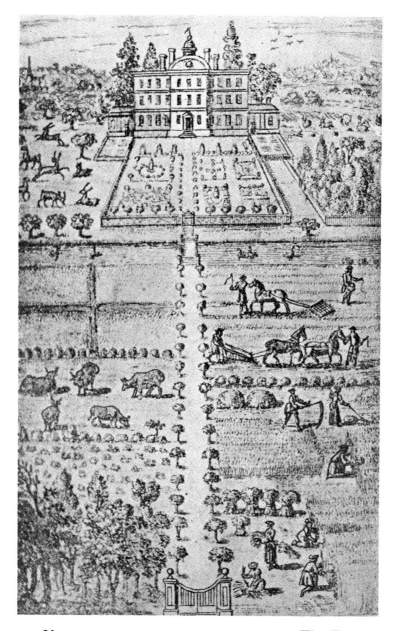

29. VARIOUS KINDS OF FARM WORK IN 1717. The Frontispiece of Giles Jacob, *The Country Gentleman's Vade Mecum*, 1717

30. THE SHEPHERD AND HIS FLOCK. From Richard
Bradley's *Gentleman's and Farmer's Guide*, 1729

This four Wheel Drill Plow, with a Seed and a Manure Hopper was first Invented in the Year 1745. and is now in Use with Wᵐ Ellis at Little Gaddesden near Hempstead in Herfordshire. where any person may View the same. It is so light that a Man may Draw it but Generally drawn by a pony or little Horse

31. FARMING IN FINE CLOTHES: trying an early seed drill. From William Ellis's *The Farmer's Instructor*, 2nd. ed., 1750

The Wall Fence planted. The Bank Fence planted.

32. (*top*): MAKING ENCLOSURES. From *A Compleat Body of Husbandry,* 1756
33. (*bottom*): A SHEPHERD AND HIS PIPE. Frontispiece to Robert Brown's *Compleat Farmer,* 1759

34. THE FARMER'S RETURN FROM MARKET. After Hogarth

35. A VISIT TO THE HORSE DOCTOR. Frontispiece from William Griffiths's *Practical Treatise on Farriery*, 1784

Arthur Young. F.R.S.
Secretary to the Board of Agriculture.
Born Sept. 7. 1741. Died. April. 12. 1820~

36. ARTHUR YOUNG. From Journal R.A.S.E., 1893.
Reproduced by courtesy of the Royal Agricultural Society
of England

37. ROBERT BAKEWELL—born 1726, died 1795. From Journal R.A.S.E., 1894

one he had discarded. He did not take into account the fact that he was not likely to need it for so long.

Most of these people had one great source of satisfaction in their lives. All the freeholders and tenants of a manor played their part in the management of village affairs by reason of their attendance at the manorial courts. Some of the functions of these courts had already been taken over by the Justices of the Peace and the local officials, but in that part of the country still farmed on the open arable field system their regulations governed the management of the farm lands.

Some of the courts made orders to control nuisances and those small pieces of venality that were so often regarded as clever and profitable tricks. At Padworth, Berkshire, orders were made in 1656 that no cattle were to be allowed to feed in the lanes. None of the farmers were "to suffer" any sheep to feed in the Eastmead on penalty of a fine of 6d. for each offence. This pasture was presumably either kept for hay or for grazing cows and oxen. Pigs at free range on the manorial commons must not be ringed. No one must surcharge the common, or, in other words, put on it a larger number of livestock than his holding allowed him to. All beasts put on the commons must be marked with the recognized town mark so that any strays from a neighbouring manor, or animals deliberately driven on to Padworth common to graze, might be impounded. The owners of these strays were fined, and the beasts sent home. The Westmead was ordered to be kept closed from the 1st March to the 1st October annually, no doubt to ensure a good crop of hay.

In another Berkshire parish the following by-laws were made at a Court Baron of the King's Manor, in East Hendred, in the year 1700. No sheep were to be allowed to feed in the West Field after the feast of All Saints (1st November) on pain of 6d. a day for each sheep. Every farmer must trench his land in the West Field on or before the feast of All Saints on pain of 1s. for every perch that stopped the water and did damage. Nobody was allowed to let any Cow common in the same year after the commons had once been stocked under a penalty of 5s. "the Common". It was ordered and agreed to set "Meerstones" on Thursday in Whitsun week. The farmers were to meet at the church porch at eight o'clock in the morning under a penalty of 2s. 6d. for absence. Meerstones were stones set up at the edge of the fields to mark the boundaries of each man's plots.

It is evident, too, that some of the farmers were none too careful of other people's property. An order was made at this Court that "every man that shall goe with his cart in the Harvest, over any lands of corn without his giving notice to the owner to cut a way for him, shall pay two shillings and sixpence for the first fault and five shillings for the second". The document was signed by Will. Wright, the Seneschal.

The open arable fields of East Hendred, like those of many of the villages lying just north of the Berkshire Downs, were divided into two great blocks. On one of these all the farmer's crops had to grow in any one year. The other lay fallow during that season. Doubtless that is why all the sheep had to be off the Westfield by the first of November in that year. Only after they had been removed could the farmers safely sow their autumn seeds.

In this village there were five manors with lands distributed about and intermixed in the great open arable fields so that there must have been quite exceptional difficulties in dealing with such a complexity of ownership and use.

All the tenants joined together at Hendred feast held here annually at the celebration of the patron saint of the church. The people of the neighbouring villages of Harwell, Steventon and Milton joined in the revels, and intended to settle outstanding disputes then. Maybe they did, but the flowing bowl that was the best part of the feast probably led to new ones. The Cat Street Revel as it was called, centred around an inn, the Royal Oak, in Cat Street. Its chief features were backsword play, wrestling and dancing for a cake. A prize of a silver-laced hat was usually presented to the winner of the backsword play. The game will be familiar to all readers of *Tom Brown's Schooldays*.

A great many of those who took part in the Cat Street Revel and other similar rejoicings in the Vale of White Horse must have been shepherds. They, in common with shepherds in other parts of the kingdom, had another festivity at the annual sheep shearing. The silver-laced hat was a sign of authority at that gathering, but its wearer gave precedence to he who wore a hat with gold lace.

The shearing in Sussex, for example, was usually done in companies, often of more than thirty men, under a captain in a gold-laced hat and a lieutenant wearing one adorned with silver. These gatherings were such a great contrast to the ordinary solitary life of a shepherd that there was every reason for a frolic, especially when the high spirits engendered by the occasion were raised by plenty of good ale. An old shepherd's song has it:

"Our shepherds rejoice in their fine heavy fleece,
And frisky young lambs, which their flocks do increase;
Each lad takes his lass
All on the green grass
Where the pink and the lily,
And the daffadowndilly . . .
Here stand our brown jug, and 'tis filled with good ale,
Our table, our table, shall increase and not fail
We'll joke and we'll sing,
And dance in a ring
Where the pink and the lily. . . ."

Women helped with the sheep shearing in both Sussex and Norfolk and probably in other places. As the song says they helped to make it a merry task as well.

On the heels of shearing came the harvest. In the lower and less hilly parts of the country this was heavy work. The grass was mowed with a scythe and it was a good mower and a strong man who could cut an acre a day. The hay was turned and windrowed and cocked by hand. Finally it was carted home and stacked close to the homestead in the stackyard or haymow. The farmers and their men, who lived in the hills of the north, Wales and the south-west, found the work so much the more difficult because of the slopes of their land. These men had to bring home the hay on sleds as in some remote parts they did until quite recently. The alternative was a packhorse. The corn, after it had been reaped, had to be transported in the same way.

In the south-west the natural difficulties were made harsher because, "In divers places . . . the ways are so rocky and narrow that it is not possible for waggons to pass, so that the Country People are forced in Harvest time to carry home their Corn upon Horses in certain Crooks made for that purpose, which creates no small Toil and Labour to them."

Celia Fiennes, too, noticed the extra hard job the farmers there had to collect their crops. She remarked that all over Devon and Cornwall hay and corn was carried on horseback and the people were obliged to support it with their hands, two to a horse, one walking on either side.

A woman led each and both the men and women toiled like their horses. The end of all this toil was, of course, celebrated in the harvest home, and then the round of the year's work began again, broken only by the fire jumping and frolicing of All Souls and the greatest festival of all, the twelve days holiday of Christmas. This was enjoyed very greatly and as greatly regretted when it had passed into the limbo of forgotten things for another year. *A Carol for Candlemas Day of 1661* declared plaintively,

> "Christmas hath made an end,
> Welladay, Welladay,
> Which was my dearest friend,
>   More is the pity.
>
> For with a heavy heart
> Must I from thee depart
> To follow plough and cart
>   All the year after.
>
> Lent is fast coming on,
> Welladay, Welladay,
> That loves not anyone,
>   More is the pity;
>
> For I doubt both my cheeks
> Will look thin eating leeks,
> Wise is he then who seeks
>   For a friend in a corner.
>
> All our good cheer is gone,
> Welladay, Welladay,
> And turned to a bone,
>   More is the pity.
>
> In my good master's house
> I shall eat no more souse,
> Then give me one carouse
>   Gentle kind butler."

There were several other occasional festivities during the year. Throwing at a cock on Shrove Tuesday, May Day, Midsummer and so on, and besides these there was the annual fair where there was a good deal of merriment, sometimes with unfortunate results. Many a rustic Phyllis regretted too late her kind complaisance at that time. Bear and bull baitings were other times when the whole village gathered round. Thomas Bellingham attended one in September 1688 that nearly had disastrous results. "Ye bull broake loose and fell down Mr. Langton's cellar stayres, and broake open the doore, and had like to have killed 2 children and ye drawyer of ye anchor." Bellingham was an enthusiast for playing bowls, hunting, fishing, paying visits, and making little jollifications at "ye anchor" where he gave parties to eat oysters on several occasions.

Many of the rural population looked upon these and all other amusements and recreations as the temptations of the devil and forsook them. There was still a large leaven of Puritanism almost everywhere in the country, though all alike did a good deal of drinking without censure. Coffee was only slowly making its way, and the tea that has now become so universal was only becoming known by an easy progression. It was heartily condemned by sticklers for tradition.

Bunyan was a type that felt it necessary to abandon such deadly sins as the wicked indulgence of bell-ringing, of playing tip-cat, of dancing, and of reading such profane works as the *History of Sir Bevis of Southampton*. He had many followers amongst country people, whose way of life was so harsh that it either moulded a severity of character no longer known, or encouraged the wildest indulgence in the seasons of festivity.

Another example of the late Stuart farmer, rather pious and thoroughly careful in all the actions of his life, is Big John Ridd, the hero of Blackmore's *Lorna Doone*. He is the type of sturdy independent farmer to be found everywhere in the country at that time. Descendants of the men who had followed Hampden and Cromwell, they had inherited many of their crude ideas, deep-rooted prejudices, and age-old superstitions. They were the tough material that was to play a large part in making England great in the following two centuries. For the time they were somewhat intractable and slow to assimilate new ways.

But indeed they were severely handicapped by the lack of informa-

F

tion. There was a literature of farming, but it probably found its way into the houses of the wealthier gentry rather than into the farmhouses. Information about market prices was limited to what could be gathered at local markets and fairs. How grateful would some of these farmers have been for the modern Weekly Market Prices. They must often have been at a loss whether to sell or hold their stocks, although there was an ever-present and immediate pressure upon them to force them to sell. They needed whatever money they could get. Consequently their bargains were often hastily and improvidently made. Harvesting was scarcely done before the produce was taken to market. Funds must be obtained to finance the work of the coming season. Banks with their credit facilities were unknown.

Under this system the farmers did their own carrying to market. The corn was transported in wagons or in carts or in "packs" on horseback. In the north it was the custom to dispatch a train of eight horseloads at a time in charge of two men. The journey occupied a long day. Sometimes an overnight stop was necessary. Wagoners, who carried their master's grain to market town, often rose at two o'clock in the morning to prepare their horses and wagons. They expected to be loaded up and ready to leave about 4 a.m. This custom lasted until well into the nineteenth century in some places. If they got back the same day, the wagons were likely to arrive long after night had fallen.

The great fairs, devoted almost exclusively to the sale and purchase of some particular article, flourished and continued to flourish until the reign of Queen Victoria. Ilsley, in a pocket of the Berkshire Downs, and now more renowned for its racing stables than anything else, was then a great corn market. A royal charter to hold a weekly market here had been granted by James I in 1620 to Sir Francis Moore. The corn market at Ilsley perhaps reached its maximum in the middle of the eighteenth century. The place, too, had been celebrated for its great sheep market, but only a few ramshackle pens remained there just before the Second World War. There were great fairs for black or neat cattle at Brough in Cumberland, at St. Faiths near Norwich, and elsewhere, and there were numerous horse fairs including that at Horncastle painted in such vivid colours by George Borrow in *Romany Rye*.

The cattle sold at Brough and other fairs in the north, as well as many of those sold at St. Faiths, were Scottish "runts" or stores, sent south to the graziers of England to be fattened mainly for the London market. There was a good deal of controversy about this trade. Some English breeders thought themselves injured by the importation of Scottish and Irish stores, and did not fail to make their voices heard.

On the one hand the Scots complained that if anything were done to put a stop to sending their beasts they would be ruined. On the other hand the Grand Jury of Yorkshire, doubtless mainly composed of the landed interest, petitioned the House of Commons in 1665 against both Scottish and Irish beasts. They declared it was the cause of "the greate wante of money and decay of trade in the County", the imported cattle

> "being fedd, maintained and fattened with farre less charge than can possibly be done in England, they fill and quit the Markets and undersell those of English breed and feeding, soe much that the ffarmers who formerly furnished other parts must and doe give over breeding and are forced to buy for themselves of that sort to their utter undoing and the Grazier cannot sell his fatt Cattle for the price they cost whereby industry is laid aside, trade decayed and put into the hands of strangers, our Coyne carried out of the Kingdome by those who buy little, if anything among us."

This petition has a rather modern sound, and perhaps to meet it and other similar complaints, if any such were made, an Act was passed in 1666, as we have already said, prohibiting the import of Irish cattle. This worried the Scots, but they had no reason to disturb themselves. Their beasts were not included in the embargo.

There is little doubt that traffic on the roads was increasing. The larger farm output that was being produced had to be carried to market, and livestock were driven from Scotland and Wales all the way to London. They may have stopped upon the way for a year or so in the hands of intermediate buyers, who fed them and passed them on at a profit. There was more industrial traffic, too.

Many of the roads were only broad tracks through the open fields and a careless driver meeting with a large pond of mud and water in the way was inclined to take to the cultivated land as easier going. The lanes leading from the farms to the highway were seas of mud in winter, and solid with hardened ruts in summer. Such maintenance as they received was provided by the farmers who used them. The ancient green tracks across the downs and hills needed no repair. Along them travelled the innumerable herds of cattle and sheep that walked to market. Solitary today except for an occasional hiker they were busy with this traffic in Stuart and Georgian times.

The main road, the public highway, was maintained by the Statute labour that each farmer was obliged to provide for a fixed number of days annually. The work was supervised by the highway surveyor, who was selected at the church vestry meeting at Easter, and served without payment until the next Easter. It was part of his duties to see that no one ploughed up the highway in order to add a foot or so to his land, or in other words to extend his boundary. Making pits in the street seems to have been another common offence. Some ingenious farmers laid straw in wet places in the road so that the passing hoofs and wheels might mangle it into a species of manure. The offence of stopping a footpath or bridle way is nothing new. For the farmer it was one way of preventing damage to his crops; for the user it was an action that spelled nothing but injustice. The most frequent user then, of course, was the local inhabitant proceeding upon his lawful occasions. The jurisdiction of the highway surveyor ended at the parish boundary. Whenever possible this official took the easy way. He was a farmer amongst farmers and next year someone else would be in the job. Naturally the surveyor in office did not press too heavily upon his neighbours for their men to work upon the roads. He did not want to be served in too harsh a way during the following year when one of his friends would have the thankless task.

The other unpaid offices the husbandman or labourer had to fill continued. Often the churchwarden was a man who could neither read nor write. He and the overseers of the poor, the highway surveyor, the constable would depend upon the parish clerk to keep their records and accounts.

Their duties were numerous and varied, and were performed with many different degrees of efficiency. They supervised the ale-houses, tried to control vagrancy and to prevent new settlements being obtained in the village. The habitual use of profane swearing was condemned and punished by them. They saw to it that all the congregation went to church as it was lawful for them to do, and they fined those who took their pleasure during the hours of divine service. The churchwardens, too, were responsible for the maintenance of the fabric of the parish church and the care of its furniture.

Other tasks that fell to the lot of this group of local officials were to inflict fines for drunkenness and to levy distress if not paid within a week. They issued licences to hawkers and pedlars. They were responsible for the burial of any unknown corpses found in the parish. They must look to the store of weapons and ammunition, kept for the use of the train bands. And they paid small rewards to those industrious persons who helped to kill off vermin ranging from polecats to rats. In their records these included eggs and heads of crows, choughs, rooks, etc., foxes and badgers' heads and a variety of other birds and animals that, rightly or wrongly, were supposed to injure either crops or stock.

The overseeing of the poor was a large business in itself, and grew more complex after the legislation of the late seventeenth century. Often a good deal more money was spent in tracing a pauper's place of settlement and sending him there than it would have cost to keep him in the village. But it would have been dangerous to let him stay. Others would have thought that parish an easy one. The overseers were supposed to force the able-bodied poor to work, and to maintain their own sick and impotent poor. A more pleasing duty was buying drink for the ringers when they gave a performance or assisted at a celebration. The officers treated themselves when supervising church repairs and so on.

Since the meetings of the parish officers took place in the vestry the character of the clergy played an important part. Few were well paid, and many were themselves farmers. Some of them engaged in the business of keeping an ale-house to supplement their stipends; others became schoolmasters. They signed the leaving certificates of workers whose employers could not write, and subscribed their names and state to the passports that allowed the unemployed to travel in search of work. They attended the frequent whippings of vagrants, female as well as male, perhaps in the capacity of village apothecary in addition to seeing that justice was fully done to these unfortunates.

The clergy, too, with a numerous company of witnesses, attended the annual Rogationtide perambulation of the parish boundaries. During this ceremony small gratuities were given to the younger people to induce them to join the procession. Children's remembrance of the marks were impressed by ducking them in streams amidst the jests and laughter of the grown-ups, bumping them against trees, and at less obvious bounds by beating them with wands.

One or more parson schoolmasters of the day, who lived near Kidderminster, were removed for flogging the boys during bouts of drunkenness. Others in that district got their living by cutting faggots, or making ropes; but the main resource of the clergy was farming their glebe and collecting their tithe.

As farmers some of the clergy were leading lights. When Mr. Russ came to the living of Mixbury in the Deanery of Bicester, Oxfordshire, little or no wheat was ever sown by the farmers. He sowed a good deal, and his example was followed by them with success.

An example of the size of holding the clergy occupied was that of the Vicar of Upton Bishop, Herefordshire. He had a house, with a barn, garden, orchard and two crofts amounting to eight acres. Certain lands and pastures called lays contained fourteen acres, and there were six acres of meadow lying together. Besides this the vicar occupied eighteen acres of arable land scattered about the three open fields, twelve acres in Linders Field, four acres called Gung Ash in Foxhill's Field, and two acres in Morrall Field.

There was no common for sheep or other cattle in this parish. Apparently the grass and meadow land was all occupied, like the vicar's in severalty, but he had tithes in the common (arable) fields of wool, flax, lambs, cyder, fruit, hemp, pigs, geese, calves and the hay, "except yᵗ groweth upon the Demayne whereof but the third part to the Vicaridge". There were also tithes here of clover, turnips, and honey, demonstrating that the new husbandry was well established before the end of Queen Anne's reign.

Tithe in kind, that thorn in the flesh of the farmer, was occasionally commuted when open fields were enclosed and made into separate farms. At Finmere in 1677 an area of 40 acres 3 roods and 25 poles was allotted to the parson, and he had two acres of Parson Holmes as well as two acres of the meadow. By this enclosure the tithe was commuted for a rent charge to be paid quarterly. It was charged upon various lands, and amounted to £80 yearly. Both the parson and his parishioners must have been pleased with this arrangement. It removed some of the continual causes of irritation consequent upon the collection of all sorts of tithes in kind throughout the year.

It did not, of course, remove the odious payment altogether. Tithe remained a bone of contention, whether paid in kind or commuted to a rent charge, until the Tithe Commutation Act of 1836, and there are still difficulties about it.

The farmer of the reign of Queen Anne accepted it with what resignation he could muster, just as he did not quail before some of the other conditions of his life that most modern Englishmen, especially townsmen, would find appalling. The farmer and his man of the first decade of the eighteenth century hardly noticed what we might consider hardships. He knew nothing else and cared for nothing else.

His work was hard and gave him small returns. Some gained greatly, but they were the fortunate few. It is difficult to generalize about farmers. Not only did their conditions of work, kinds of work, and of living, housing and so on, vary widely between the different parts of the kingdom, but as always there were often wealthy and poverty-stricken farmers in the same county; the same parish.

Physical and climatical conditions, soil, elevation, and slope all made it necessary for farmers in, say Cornwall and Devon, Cumberland and Northumberland, Cheshire and East Anglia to use methods and systems that had been developed by experience gained since the land was settled. Naturally this practice was alike in some respects, but in many particulars of management very dissimilar. "Of no age is this more obviously true," it has been said, "than of the seventeenth century, when a small minority outstripped their contemporaries in cultivation." This was no less true in farming circles than it was in the realms of poetry and religion to which the remark referred. All those changes in the work and living of the farmers that began in this period wrought a revolution in the eighteenth century, a revolution that affected very intimately all classes of rural society.

Though poets had sung the praises of country life for centuries before this time, already a tinge of realism was to be found in some of the pastoral poetry and prose of that day. Everybody knows the romantic tales the *Spectator* told about Sir Roger de Coverley. Many know Gay's *Shepherd's Week*; but possibly Pope's criticism of the pastoral poetry of his time is not so familiar. He thought the pastoral poets aimed at producing an image of the golden age. They did not describe the shepherds as they really were at that time, but as they may be conceived to have been when the best of men followed the employment.

Pungently he added that nothing conduces to make these composures natural than when some knowledge of rural affairs is discovered. It was the tranquillity rather than the business of a country life that appealed to the reader. The poet must use some illusion exposing the best side only of a shepherd's life and concealing its miseries.

But we doubt whether the men of the land concerned themselves very much about pastoral poetry or its theories. They went on in their accustomed round, working hard most of the time, and eating and living frugally. At the traditional times of holiday and feasting they abandoned the restraints of ordinary days and enjoyed themselves with a heartiness we have forgotten how to feel. The measure of their occasional junketings was the measure of the normal dourness of their lives.

CHAPTER FOUR

The Farmer under the Hanovers, 1714–1792

THE *Spectator* wrote a halcyon description of paternal country life in the first years of the eighteenth century. Sir Roger de Coverley was his ideal of an elderly country gentleman who ruled his neighbourhood and estate with a firm but kindly hand. Everyone loved and admired Sir Roger, and no one would have dreamed of opposing his amiable tyrannies.

Unlike many of his contemporaries Sir Roger was a man of equable temper and untroubled mind. In his youth he had been a great sportsman. He had hunted, fished and shot with the best just as so many of the landowning gentry and yeomen continued to do for nearly two centuries more.

His estates were tenanted by people who had served him as domestics and personal servants. Their ancestors had served his ancestors in the same way for generations. They were as simple as he was himself. Once when a milkmaid came home in a frenzy and declared that she had been terrified by a headless ghost, Sir Roger could not disbelieve her. Three parts of his house were shut up because the rooms were haunted. Everyone knew there were ghosts and apparitions, hobgoblins and will-o'-the-wisps.

Sir Roger's chaplain was a man who possessed plain sense, a clear voice and a sociable temper. Sir Roger made him play backgammon because he "feared to be insulted with Latin and Greek at his own table". He felt that his people (the villagers) would soon degenerate into savages if they did not go to church. He made them attend regularly, and ruled the whole congregation as he ruled them in daily life. Nobody was allowed to sleep through the sermon except Sir Roger. If he woke and saw anybody nodding, he would wake them himself, or send his servant to do so. Occasionally he would stand up when everyone else was kneeling. He counted them to discover if anyone was missing. He went out of church first, and greeted everyone on the porch. When he died, it was the most melancholy day for the poor people that ever happened in Worcestershire.

In many places this sort of paternal autocracy continued until well into the nineteenth century. Sir Roger was a type. Innumerable squires played his part though not all of them were so amiable. They were used to ruling in their own small realms. This enabled them to take the lead in improved farming, if they were improvers. They could easily persuade their tenants to follow their example, or they could bring pressure to bear if a tenant was unwilling to adopt the new methods.

Farming, the profession of most of the squirearchy after the Restoration, became a rage with some large landowners in the early years of the Hanover dynasty. Foremost amongst them was Lord Townshend, who had led the first government of George I as Secretary of State, only to become second fiddle to Walpole in 1721, after the bursting of the South Sea Bubble. Nine years later Walpole succeeded in driving Townshend out of office. In dudgeon he retired to his country seat in Norfolk to indulge the agricultural pursuits that made him famous as "Turnip Townshend". Had fortune turned the other way, it might as easily have been Walpole who was driven back to country life to earn the sobriquet. Had he not come to London seeking political fortune, a young Norfolk landowner, whose "big square figure, vulgar good-humoured face were those of a common country squire", he would have spent his life farming the family estate.

From this time farming enthusiasm spread like wildfire amongst the great landowners. Before the French Revolution they were everywhere busily engaged in improving their estates. When the King himself (George III) became a practical improving farmer everybody who was anybody followed his example. George III never travelled without the latest volume of Arthur Young's *Annals of Agriculture* in his coach. He admired this periodical so much that, thinly disguised under the pseudonym, "Ralph Robinson", the name of his shepherd at Windsor, he contributed many a page to it. This King loved to be called "Farmer George".

Between 1714 and 1792 many were added to the names famous as men of the land. Others unknown to fame played their part amongst them. The wealthy Nabobs, who had made fortunes in India were some. They came home to buy great estates, for land hunger was the understandable appetite of these gentry. An investment in land was profitable and became more profitable as the century advanced; it provided an attractive residence that great wealth could readily modernize; it gave a high social position and might supply a ready means of getting into Parliament. Great houses like Haldon House, Devon; Park Place Farm, Eltham; Stansted, Sussex; Basildon, Berks; Patshull, Stafford; White Knights, near Reading; and Woodhall Park, Wotton Woodhall, Herts, all owe much to the wealth of the Indies.

In some places the rebuilding or extension of the great house involved moving a hamlet to another site. This happened at Milton Abbas in Dorset, Nuneham Courtenay in Oxfordshire, and Stowe.

At Milton Abbas the old hamlet, just outside the garden wall of the great house, was demolished. A new model village was built; a wide street with pairs of cottages on both sides. Small gardens were provided, and chestnut trees, now very magnificent, were planted. Unfortunately the cottages soon became very overcrowded. The pretty scene concealed a good deal of discomfort, some real misery. At Nuneham Courtenay the villagers were moved into two rows of new brick cottages built along the road from Henley to Oxford. At Stowe the people were sent to Dadford.

The new farming was introduced at Milton Abbas. From 1760 onwards large quantities of clover seed were bought at intervals. Mr. Freeman of Fawley Court supplied the first lot of 1,120 lb. of Dutch seed. For the profitable cultivation of clover, of turnips and the other new forage crops, the ideal practice of the "improvers", enclosed fields held in individual occupation and subject to no rights of common grazing were essential. The open-field system had to go whatever injustices its abolition might involve. "Reformers" like Arthur Young, who began his celebrated tours in 1767, were never weary of calling for its abolition, and with it of the common pastures. Enclosure had never absolutely ceased since Tudor times, but now it began with fresh ardour; and between 1760 and 1850 by means of the Enclosure Acts, practically all the remaining open fields and most of the commons were swept away. Jeremy Bentham, the utilitarian philosopher, thought the spectacle of an enclosure, "one of the most reassuring of all the evidences of improvement and happiness", but Young, despite his earlier enthusiasm in support of the movement, admitted later that "By nineteen out of twenty Enclosure Bills the poor are injured and some grossly injured. The poor in these parishes may say with truth, 'All I know is I had a cow and an Act of Parliament has taken it from me'. A man will love his country better even for a pig". It was the enclosure of the waste that most particularly affected the cottagers and the poor. By consent, or by right, they had been allowed to graze on the wild grass of the waste what livestock they could acquire, a few poultry or a cow, a shaggy ass or a pony and they might cut furze or turf for fuel, rights that disappeared upon enclosure.

But not all new farms were made at the expense of the people, nor was reclamation work all done by great landowners. Some new farms were made out of the unused waste, or waste that was only used by the lonely shepherd to graze his widely wandering flocks. Some of the work, too, was done by tenant farmers whose holdings were very large.

Arthur Young, writing in 1768, about what he had seen in the previous few years, described what had already been done in part of Norfolk.

"All the country from *Holkham* to *Houghton* was a wild sheep walk before the spirit of improvement seized upon the inhabitants; and this glorious spirit has wrought amazing effects; for instead of boundless wilds and uncultivated wastes, inhabited by scarce anything but sheep; the country is all cut into enclosures, cultivated in a most husbandmanlike manner, richly manured, well peopled, and yielding an hundred times the produce that it did in its former state. What has wrought these vast improvements is the marling; for under the whole country runs veins of very rich soapy kind, which they dig up, and spread upon the old sheep walks, and then by means of enclosing they throw their farms into a regular course of crops, and gain immensely by the improvement.

The farms are all large and the rents low, for the farmers having

38. (*above*): FARM LABOURER'S
FAMILY AND COTTAGE. From
an illustration to Crabbe's
Poems (1858 edition)

39. "The pliant bow he
formed, the flying ball.

The bat, the wickets were
his labours all".

From Crabbe's *Poems* (1858
edition)

40. "The Penny Wedding." From an engraving of a painting by Sir David Wilkie. A wedding feast of this kind is described by Thomas Hardy

41. (*above*): REAPING. An illustration to a quotation from Clare's *Shepherds' Calendar*
42. "The quiet of a summer's eve," Clare's *Shepherds' Calendar*. The mower takes his pipe and tankard beside his own doorstep and fondly watches his children play

43. RURAL SPORT. "The Ass Race." After George Morland

44. A FARMYARD—master and man. From *The Compleat Farmer,*
4th edition, 1793

45. Ploughman at work. From John Boys's *General View of the Agriculture of Kent,* 1796

46. (*top*): MEN AT WORK. Hoeing by man-power and using an early type of hay collector. From *Rural Recollections, or Modern Farmer's Calendar*, by a farmer, 1802

47. (*bottom*): CHIGNAL SMEALEY. A farmyard near Chelmsford, Essex. From an old engraving in the author's possession

48. An English rat-catcher from a contemporary engraving

49. THE SUSSEX TRUFFLE HUNTER a hundred years ago. From an early nineteenth-century engraving

50. FRONTISPIECE from Francis Clater's *Every Man His Own Farrier*, 21st ed., 1812

51. JOHN ELLMAN of Glynde, Sussex. From Baxter's *Library of Agricultural and Horticultural Knowledge*, 1836

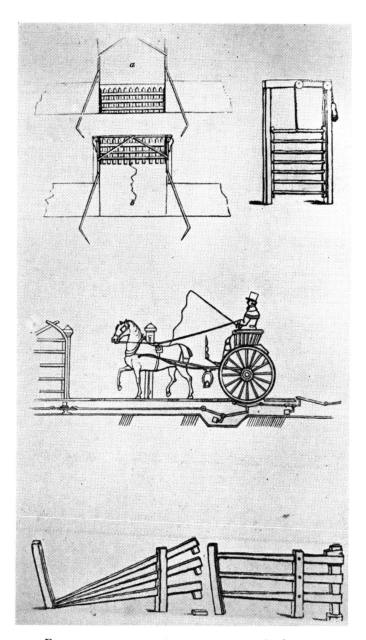

52. ENCLOSURE meant new gates and fences: the
sympathetic gate. The stile of falling bars. From J. C.
Loudon, *Encyclopaedia of Agriculture*, 1825

53. THE STATUTE FAIR in decline. Hiring servants in the late Georgian period. From a nineteenth-century print

54. A BOOTH AT STOURBRIDGE FAIR. This was a very large fair, but booths of this kind, though perhaps not so large, were put up at most fairs. From a nineteenth-century engraving

55. (*top*): THE NEW AND IMPROVED BRIDESTON COTTAGES. From
Charles Vancouver, *General View of the Agriculture of Devon*, 1808
56. (*bottom*): A FARMER, homeward bound, paying the toll at a
country toll-gate. From an unsigned water-colour (early nineteenth
century) in the author's collection

57. AT HOME IN THE EVENING: after Sir David Wilkie. "The Rabbit on the Wall," 1816

been at a great expense in improvements, they could not afford
them without very long leases."

These lucky men had their farms at less than they were really
worth. The landlords, "who had a vanity in not raising their rents"
a peculiar and much to be admired species of pride, encouraged them.
Consequently many of the farmers had been able to make their
fortunes and some were able to buy their farms. This development
was all across the country from Holkham to the sea westward and south
to Swaffham. It happened before Coke decided to live at Holkham.

Among the great farmers were Mr. Curtis of Sommerfield, and Mr.
Mallet of Dunton, each of whom occupied 2,500 acres. Messrs. Glovers
of Creek and Barwic, Savary of Sydderstone, and Rogerson of Narford,
each occupied 1,100 acres. Young is not very explicit about the methods
by which all this was achieved, and there is a good deal yet to learn
about it, but it is known that on the Townshend estates at Raynham
enclosures were being made for arable farming and marl was being
spread to make the land fit for it so early as 1661. Early in the eighteenth
century turnips were extensively grown on the estate, clover and
sainfoin was planted, Scotch heifers were bought and careful attention
was paid to dairy farming though Charles, Lord Townshend, did not
devote his whole energies to farming until after 1733. Thus was the
pattern of west Norfolk improved farming laid down. When in 1776
the famous Coke of Norfolk inherited his estate of 43,000 acres at
Holkham, to become a more famous leader in agricultural development, he was able to follow in these inspired footsteps.

These large tenant farmers, the yeoman of their day, lived in fine
style as their means allowed. Their houses, many of which are still
occupied, were large and substantial, and their furniture and clothing
of the best. Naturally, too, their food was all that they could desire.

Arthur Young, possibly with a bias towards optimism, estimated
the annual profit of a farm of 1,100 acres in this part of Norfolk at
£1,263 "on a medium of prices and seasons". When he was writing
there had been four or five wet years, and this was an advantage to
these light land farmers. He thought that the profit had been more
than doubled in some of those years and might have reached £3,000
at times. This is still a large income and was then very large. It was as
much or more than that of many a landowner, and made a tenant

farmer, who paid only about a shilling a day for his labour, a wealthy man. One of them, Mr. Mallet, was able to buy estates in the parishes of Middletone, Testerton and Hockham that returned a rental of £1,700 a year.

Men of this type, whose ancestors had been proud of the designation, yeoman, came to be enviously called gentlemen farmers, by their less enterprising and successful neighbours. Crabbe has drawn a sketch of such a one that can hardly be improved upon.

> "Gwyn was a farmer, whom the farmers all,
> Who dwelt around, the *Gentleman* would call;
> Whether in pure humility or pride,
> They only knew and they would not decide.
> Far different he from that dull plodding tribe,
> Whom it was his amusement to describe;
> Creatures no more enlivened than a clod,
> But treading still as their dull father's trod;
> Who lived in times when not a man had seen
> Corn sown by drill, or threshed by a machine;
> He was of those whose skill assignes the prize
> For creatures fed in pen, or stall or sties;
> And who, in places where improvers meet,
> To fill the land with fatness had a seat;
> Who in large mansions live like petty Kings,
> And speak of farms but as amusing things
> Who plans encourage, and who journals keep.
> And talk with lords about a breed of sheep.
> Two are the species in this genus known;
> One, who is rich in his profession grown,
> Who yearly finds his ample stores increase
> From fortune's favours and a favouring lease;
> Who rides his hunter, who his house adorns;
> Who drinks his wine, and his disbursements scorns;
> Who freely lives and loves to show he can.
> This is my farmer made the gentleman.
> The second species from the world is sent,
> Tired with its strife, or with his wealth content;
> In books and men beyond the former read,

To farming solely by a passion bid,
Or by a fashion, curious in his land;
Now planning much, now changing what he planned;
Pleased by each trial nor by failures vex'd
And ever certain to succeed the next;
Quick to resolve and easy to persuade,
This is the gentleman farmer made."

Crabbe was born in Suffolk and was writing about conditions in his own neighbourhood. Far away in the south-west, if we can believe Thomas Day, there were enterprising farmers in Devonshire. Already ploughing matches had been organized there to stimulate skill in the men and to compare the performance of different implements. Farmer Sandford, rejecting Mr. Merton's proferred gift of money, declared,

"When I was a young man, and that is nearly forty years ago (i.e. about 1740) farmers did not lie droning in bed as they do now till six or seven; my father, I believe, was as good a judge of business as any in the neighbourhood, and turned as straight a furrow as any ploughman in the county of Devon; that silver cup, which I intend to have the honour of drinking your health out of today at dinner, that very cup was won by him at a great ploughing match near Axminster."

Men like these did not live very differently from the small squires, the little independent gentlemen of three hundred a year or so, who were supposed by some to have quite vanished from the rural scene by the end of the eighteenth century. These admired characters usually wore a plain drab or plush coat adorned with silver buttons, a jockey cap and riding boots. They rarely travelled farther than the neighbouring market town where they made it a habit to dine once a week with their fellow justices and the local attorneys. This the farmers did as well, but ate in the company of their compeers at the market ordinary provided by one or other of the inns. The squire might go as far as the county town for the assizes or at an election. He attended his parish church regularly, kept himself in touch with affairs by reading the weekly journal, and acted as arbitrator in parochial disputes between the parish officers at the vestry, afterwards getting drunk at the local ale-house "for the good of the country". Ale was his drink by ordinary but he would brew a brandy punch at Christmas, a birthday, or some occasion like 5th November. When he visited a neighbour he was followed by a pair of greyhounds and a pointer, and announced himself by smacking his whip and a loud view hallo.

The house of a squire of this degree might very well have been a farmhouse, as indeed it was, because the squire himself was a farmer. It was built of local materials, timber framing and plaster, sometimes called callimaco work, or red brick with large casemented bow windows, a porch with seats in it and a so-called study above it.

The hall, just as in a farmhouse, was garnished with flitches of bacon. Guns, fishing rods and all the sporting gear of the day, adorned the mantelpiece and walls. Added ornament was provided by pasting up King Charles's Golden Rules, Vincent Wing's Almanack, and a portrait of the Duke of Marlborough. The window seat held his literature, Baker's *Chronicle*, Fox's *Book of Martyrs*, Glanvil on *Apparitions*, Quincey's *Dispensatory*, *The Complete Justice* and a book of farriery, the last doubtless frequently referred to. In this chamber he took his ease enthroned in a large wooden two-armed chair.

Life lived in this way sounds very primitive, but it was often a life of comfort, almost luxury, and some of these apparently primitive people were essentially civilized. Matthew Bramble, a fictional Welsh squire, fully appreciated the advantages derived from his country life. He had elbow room within doors and breathed a clean healthy air. His sleep was sound in the rural quiet. His food and drink was not contaminated or fixed up. Water from a limpid spring or home-brewed ale was his beverage, with an occasional bottle of imported claret. His bread was made from his own wheat, ground in his own mill, and baked at home. His table was almost entirely provided from his own farm and he declared that his five-year-old mutton would vie with venison, while his milk-fed veal filled the dish with gravy. His poultry, game, rabbits and fish came to the table almost directly they were killed. Milk and cream, butter and cheese were the produce of his own dairy, and good hams and bacon were the yield of pigs fed partly on dairy waste. The orchard and garden supplied fresh fruit and vegetables. He cared for his tenants, superintended his farm, and made cautious improvements. In inclement weather he amused himself with billiards, cards or backgammon. He says nothing about the pleasures of reading, but no doubt he indulged in that time-absorbing pursuit.

Some of the Suffolk yeomen possessed a good many books, though whether they spent any large amount of time in reading them is quite another matter. The books may have been looked upon as heirlooms, something to be passed down from hand to hand, rather than to be used to destruction by too frequent handling.

Arthur Partridge, yeoman and tenant farmer of Shelley Hall, near Stowmarket, Suffolk, who died in 1789, possessed a small library. The books issued before his death that have come down to his descendants, though they may not all have been his, amount to thirty-eight volumes. Several are devotional or theological, and include Fox's *Abridgement*, 1589, besides works issued in the seventeenth and eighteenth centuries. Gerard's *Herbal* of 1579 with the illustrations is a treasure, and may have been used by the women of this household for copying embroidery patterns. There is a copy of *Dictionarium Rusticum and Urbanicum* of 1704, an early farming and domestic encyclopaedia. A book on reading, writing and arithmetic, a ready reckoner on interest calculations, and one on the art of gauging. A little-known book on farriery by George Fisher, and the *Spectacle de la Nature* were both published in 1740. The absorbing interest of this man in his profession is denoted by William Halfpenny's *Twelve beautiful designs for farmhouses*, 1747, and Joseph Shaw's *Practical Justice of the Peace*, 1751; Burns's book of 1764 on the same subject is also present. *The Guardian* in two volumes, 1751, books on history and domestic medicine are others, but this list is too long to give *in extenso*.

Sam Blyth, who farmed at Great Wigborough in Essex, died in 1796. He owned about twenty books of different kinds, including a large Bible, Barnard's *History of England, Tristam Shandy*, Salmon's *Gazeteer* (of England and Wales) and an English Dictionary.

The similarity between these two men's books in number and kind is most likely an indication that they were characteristic of their class, and that small libraries like these were usual in the homes of well-to-do yeoman farmers.

The only other literate people in the villages and hamlets were the clergy and many of these were like Mr. Trulliber, a parson on Sundays, but more probably a farmer all the rest of the week. The Church was, in fact, in no high condition in the eighteenth century.

G

The stipends were often so minute that it was only by farming the glebe that the village clergy could hope to eke out a scanty living. There is a story of one who cultivated a churchyard, and on being rebuked by his bishop did not submit meekly. The bishop hoped that he would not see clover grown for hay in the churchyard next year. The parson adroitly replied that he would not, wheat was the proper crop.

Trulliber, one of these farming parsons, was found by Parson Adams,

"stript into his waistcoat, with an apron on, and a pail in his hand, just come from serving his hogs. He occupied a small piece of land of his own, besides which he rented a considerable deal more. His wife milked his cows, managed his dairy and followed the market with butter and eggs. The hogs fell chiefly to his care, which he carefully waited on at home and attended to at fairs; on which occasion he was liable to many jokes, his own size being, with much ale, rendered little inferior to that of the beasts he sold."

As a concession to his visitor he doffed his apron and donned an old nightgown, his customary dress for receiving guests at home.

Trulliber contrasts unfavourably with the gentle "Vicar of Wakefield", but was to be preferred to the cynical Mr. Patten, curate of Whitstable, who, to rate it lowly, "was not a very rigid high priest. He openly kept a mistress and on anyone going into church in sermon time and showing him a lemon, he would instantly conclude his discourse and adjourn to the ale house". There were, of course, distinguished and scholarly churchmen even in that age, but it is doubtful whether they were numbered amongst those who served in the tiny isolated villages.

Drinking was excessive amongst all classes both in town and country, and wild parties especially in the winter were not unusual. A Sussex diarist of the time records that the chief diversions of people were drunkeness, sexuality and horseplay. The winter evenings were either spent at home playing a card game called brag, or visiting neighbours and drinking like horses. Men and women alike got rapidly drunk, and then began dancing or jumping about and drinking all the time as fast as it could be poured down. The parson of the parish was one amongst this multitude.

The yeomen of Sussex were apparently well-to-do as were their neighbours in Kent where a foreigner noticed that they were "commonly on Horseback, in Riding Coats and Plush Breeches, booted and spurred and always galloping. . . . The People in general are well cloathed, which is a certain proof of their living at Ease, for in *England* the Belly always takes place of the Back." Midway through the century these men wore good cloth of plain and decent cut, but a Swedish traveller was amused to see every man, farm servant, clodhopper, day labourer and farmer, all going about their everyday work with peruques upon their heads, very few wearing their own hair. The wagoners of Kent, like the farmers, always impressed foreigners with their appearance of opulence.

Wagoners dressed comfortably. They were either labourers or small husbandmen driving wagons loaded with corn to market. They dressed in good cloth, each with a warm greatcoat on his back and good boots upon his legs. They rode upon a little nag, not upon the wagon itself. A farmer and his wife were so opulent in appearance that they were mistaken for a gentleman and lady, a very embarrassing mistake to be sure.

The improved farming that was characteristic of East Anglia, Kent, and part of other Home Counties by the date of Young's first tour, was equalled in the north some twenty years later. Sir Thomas Bernard was greatly impressed in August, 1780. No other country exceeded Northumberland in the spirit of wisdom and improvement. "Luxuriant Plantations, neat Hedges, rich crops of Corn, comfortable Farm Houses and elegant Mansions rise and adorn the country, the greater part whereof was barren Moor, dearly rent at 18 Pence an Acre, about 30 Years ago; when Cultivation and Building were ranked amongst their natural or artificial Curiosities." Unfortunately in neighbouring Durham a too enthusiastic use of lime had often done more harm than good. When he visited Salop the good knight thought that a few Northumberland farmers would be of great service in quickening the wits of honest Shropshire farmers. Their country was fertile by nature, though very little assisted by art, but then they had not to overcome the obstacles that had confronted those who settled in Northumberland. For example when the father of the famous John Grey of Dilston first settled in Glendale "the plain was a forest of wild broom. He took his axe and, like a backwoodsman, cleared a space on which to begin his farming operations. The country was then wholly unenclosed, without roads or signposts. Cattle were lost for days in the broom forests. The inhabitants, were as wild as their home—the Cheviot herdsmen ferocious and sullen, the rural population uneducated, ill clothed and barbarous."

The work was perhaps assisted by the local custom of paying labour partly in kind. It has often been described and lingered until well into the nineteenth century on both sides of the border, Sir Thomas Bernard wrote,

"The cottager has his cottage, a certain measure of corn, the run of one or two cows, of four or five sheep and two or three pigs; besides this he has 6d. a day during harvest from year to year;—and all this on condition of his working for the farmer at certain periods fixed by the custom of the farms.

By these means the tenant has all the necessaries of life within himself; and the farmer can command a sufficient number of labourers for every exigency. The farmer from whom we had our information held a farm of £490 a year; and had under him of vassaled labourers fifty persons; his blacksmith held a cottage and certain privileges, on condition of shoeing his cattle, being found iron."

Slowly, too, in Lancashire, where society was still very primitive, and wheat "about forty or fifty years since (i.e. before 1710) as great a Stranger in this Parish (Warton) as it is now in either *Denmark* or *Barbary*" was just displacing the old bread crops of oats and barley. The houses at Warton were thatched as they were in so many other parts of the country, the poorer ones here with bracken. Some were open to the roof, and some, possibly a curiosity, still without a chimney.

Farmers in places far distant from the capital were introducing new methods, but it was in the Home Counties, East Anglia and the east Midlands where the new crops were first cultivated. The yearly alternation between a crop for men and a crop for animals had at length solved the whole problem of winter keep. The enclosure of the open arable fields and much of the waste made it possible to begin selective breeding. The new cropping discoveries initiated a cycle of growth. Better supplies of forage enabled farmers to maintain their flocks and herd in good condition through the winter.

They did not have to kill them off in autumn. Flocks and herds became more numerous and the inferior stock could be weeded out so that only the best need be kept for breeding. More stock, cattle wintered in yards, or sheep in the fold, provided more manure and their better food made the residue richer. More and better manure stimulated plant growth, and gave better yields of heavier grain, grass and roots. In fact everything worked together for good in those fortunate places where the farmers were sensible enough to adopt the new farming, where farms were held "in several", or enclosed fields either on a long lease or other secure tenure or ownership, and where the farmers themselves had or could obtain sufficient capital to proceed upon the most advantageous lines.

All over the Midland Counties from Westmorland and Lancashire across Yorkshire, south through the Marcher Counties and eastwards to Lincoln, the cattle were much the same, though many counties claimed a breed of their own, generically known as neat, or black cattle. They were not large, and had wide-spreading horns so that they came to be known as the longhorn breed, as distinct from the middlehorns of Gloucester, Hereford, Devon and Sussex, and the shorthorns that so far were confined to the eastern seaboard counties of Lincoln and Yorkshire.

So early as 1720 Sir Thomas Gresley of Drakelow near Burton-on-Trent possessed an outstanding herd of longhorn cattle. From these a blacksmith and farrier named Welby, who lived at Linton in Derbyshire just on the borders of Leicester, developed a herd of pure and improved cattle that made a name locally, if not farther afield. His experiments were ended tragically by an outbreak of disease which defied all remedial measures then known and half ruined him. This simple man deserves to be remembered in spite of his failure from outrageous fortune.

Another farmer took up where Welby was forced to leave off. Mr. Webster of Canley, near Coventry, distinguished himself as a breeder, using foundation stock from the Drakelow herd and bulls from Lancashire and Westmorland, so that his herd came to be regarded as the best stock that ever were or ever would be bred in the kingdom. One of Webster's bulls was sold and passed through several hands before being bought in again. It was named Bloxedge and must have had a great effect on the local herds.

Robert Bakewell, born in 1725, followed Webster of Canley. He has become greatly renowned both as a breeder of longhorn cattle, the originator of the New Leicester sheep, and a farmer of great initiative in all ways.

Nothing much is known of Welby, but a great deal is known about Bakewell, who farmed at Dishley Grange for forty years from 1755 to 1795. Bakewell was, of course, fortunate in his time. Improved farming was becoming the hobby of great landowners. Wide publicity was secured by the improving farmers and breeders through such people as Arthur Young. With this spreading interest Bakewell became renowned.

In appearance he was a real John Bull with a weather-beaten jovial visage, broad shoulders, hearty manner and stout frame of an English yeoman. His dress was the loose brown coat, leather breeches, top boots and flattish wide-brimmed hat of the English yeoman. His manners in a day of stiff and formal courtesy were considered impeccable. But he showed the independence of his class after he had become world famous, and was visited by the nobility and gentry of Europe and the wealthy democracy of America, by retaining the simple everyday routine of a well-to-do grazier.

"At midday on the hard benches of his kitchen every grade of social distinction was to be found partaking of his famous mutton and beef. His parlour walls had resounded with the admiring expressions of every European tongue. He had talked farming shop to German Highnesses and Russian Counts by the score, but to the last he remained that strange mixture of simplicity and shrewdness which is the unique possession of the British Farmer."

After dinner visitors were taken out to see the cattle displayed by two veteran herds, John Breedon and William Arnold, who worked for Bakewell for thirty-two and twenty years. William Peet, older and of longer service, showed the fine horses in the stables. Punctilious regularity governed every arrangement on the farm. At eight Bakewell breakfasted, at one he dined, at nine he supped, at eleven he went to bed, whoever might be his guests. His beasts lived as regular a life, and were as healthy as their master.

Many followed and paralleled Bakewell's example. Fowler of Rollright, Oxfordshire, Princep of Croxall in Derby, Paget of Ibstock, Leicestershire, and the Culleys and the Collinges for shorthorns. The Herefords and Devons, too, had their famous breeders.

Bakewell had perfected the New Leicester sheep. John Ellman of Glynde in Sussex perfected the Southdown. He was born at Hartfield, Sussex, in 1753, whence his father moved to the Home Farm, Glynde, in 1761. John succeeded to this farm in 1780, two years after his father had begun breeding improved Southdowns, an enterprise in which he was assisted by the Duke of Bedford, Coke of Norfolk, and other noblemen. John continued and improved upon his father's work earning from Arthur Young the soubriquet "this incomparable farmer", the flock being equally praised as unrivalled.

The Duke of Bedford often stayed at Glynde. He would desert the gay parties of the Prince of Wales at Brighton to ride over the Downs and study farming with Ellman. His arrival was not dreaded as that of a fastidious peer. He was welcomed by every member of the household, and was content to live in the style of his hosts, waited upon at table by maids in place of the numerous flunkeys who attended upon his meals at Woburn Abbey. We think it is doubtful whether the noble duke ate his food in the company of the labouring servants who lived in the house in the old-fashioned way until Ellman's retirement. He died in 1852.

Great farmers like Bakewell and Ellman, who hob-nobbed with princelings and nobility, were the unusual. By the end of the eighteenth century less famous men of their class were scattered throughout the country from Northumberland to Wiltshire, from Devon to East Anglia. They were the exception and not the rule. Then as always the majority of farms were small. The men who farmed them lived labourious days in a lifelong struggle to wrest a bare living from their holdings. Not for them the excitement of experimental farming. Life was enough of a gamble for them if they followed the traditional way, the accepted canon. True the great prizes gained by the more speculative of the highly capitalized farmers eluded them, but their wants were few and simple. They were satisfied when the seasons proved favourable enough to enable them to pay their rent and to keep sufficient in hand to begin the next year's work without undue anxiety.

Prices of corn were low before 1760, and often there were loud complaints of agricultural depression. Farmers said that they could not pay their rents, small gentry were obliged to sell their estates, great landlords were compelled by loss of income to curtail their establishments. After 1770, too, the national production of corn failed to meet the requirements of the increasing population and there was no surplus for export. The home growth indeed had to be supplemented by imports, small and irregular at first, but becoming larger and continuous as time passed.

All these conditions pressed hardly upon the small man. Farming had become more risky and speculative than ever. Only the wealthy man could hold his harvest for a rise; the poor man must sell as soon as the grain was threshed for whatever it would realize. He had to have money. Even those small farmers who continued to rely mainly upon cattle breeding and dairy farming found themselves in serious difficulties and their business became less remunerative as the century drew to its close.

In Kent where clover and sainfoin were grown by the enterprising it was perhaps the small farmers who grew rye, partly for sale and partly to mix with wheat to grind and make bread of it. Kalm, who observed this practice also saw extensive fields of rye grown in Essex, but was told that only poor people used it for bread there.

There has been a great controversy about the extent to which wheaten bread was eaten and the number of people who used rye, a mixture of rye and wheat, or even barley bread and oatcake and so on. All of these things were eaten in the form of bread, bannocks or oatcake until the end of the eighteenth century in different parts of the country, often by the small farmer and labourer alike; but the exact ratio in which the different grains were used has not so far been precisely determined.

There has always been one advantage to farming, especially of the mixed type so general in the eighteenth century. Much of the food eaten is home grown. John Baker of Horsham, Sussex, when on a visit in 1771, "ate some bacon and eggs and mutton chops and drank tea and had some hot brandy punch and came away at ½ past 4". In May the following year he had for dinner "makrell" brought from Brighton. Again in May 1773 he dined on "mullet, very good, with a little cold mutton and asparagus". A great deal of salt meat was eaten and caused the prodigious thirsts that only copious draughts of strong ale, wine and spirits could assuage. Pickled pork was the mainstay during the winter, from necessity, not choice. It was prepared by steeping in brine. In Sussex "after being thus pickled, somewhat in the Egyptian manner, they slice it off when cured as the family may want", remarked a visiting medico. "They also cook a certain lump of barley meal, looking much like mud itself, and hardened like iron, offering it at meals instead of bread. These you will find universally." In 1757 Thomas Turner of East Hoathly declared he would only eat twice a day and then pudding because it was such a bad year. The returns from his labours were so meagre as to fill him with dismay.

In Bedfordshire at a later date most of the farmers that were not very poor were in the habit of purchasing some joint of meat for the Sabbath Day at least. A budget of the weekly cost of the common diet of this class included 2 lb of salted pork, 1 lb. of cheese, $\frac{1}{2}$ lb. of butter, $\frac{1}{2}$ lb. of sugar, 1 oz. of tea, 1 lb. 4 oz. of bread or common pudding, $\frac{1}{2}$ gallon of skimmed milk, and $1\frac{1}{2}$ pints small beer and 1 pint of ale daily, an abstemious regimen in all truth.

One article of diet that had previously been almost unknown came into fairly wide use in some parts of the country during the eighteenth century. It was the humble potato that is now so everyday a dish. In Lancashire and in the south-western counties it was extensively grown, though there were many who condemned it then and later. For example Samuel Oldknow ploughed out a deal of grass and set potatoes during the month of May 1788 presumably to supply the need of his "hands". Potato growing was by then an integral part of farming in parts of Lancashire and Cheshire, and potato ground was often part of the emoluments of the labourer in Dorset and Devon.

When John Ellman entertained the Duke of Bedford his grace showed no disposition to criticize the farmhouse furniture in spite of the contrast it made with the splendour of his own home. This is not so surprising as it seems. A contemporary picture of the "Installation Supper as given at the Pantheon, by the Knights of the Bath on the 26th May, 1788" shows how little the great and wealthy of the day demanded in the way of comfort upon such an occasion. Hard seats on benches, plain tables with no plate or floral decorations, and no napkins, were apparently quite acceptable.

The furniture in the living-room of a farmhouse or country inn was a long oak table, sometimes dating from Jacobean times, possibly discarded from a more important house and a contemporary oak table with straight cylindrical legs united by stretchers. There was an oak dresser, with or without superstructure of shelves and cupboards, an article greatly valued by modern taste. On this were the old pewter and possibly the new earthenware plates that were within the financial reach of modest households by 1770. A corner cupboard and an oak clock, a wooden armchair, perhaps with a cushioned seat, for the master, and a similar chair with smaller arms for the mistress, with some benches completed the tale. If there were a few books they would be in the window seat, and the mantelpiece was probably adorned by a mirror. A great many inventories of the household goods of farmers have been printed, and all confirm these descriptions.

Miss Jekyll used the popular Toby Jug from which to describe the eighteenth-century farmer, with knee-breeches, three-cornered hat, flowered waistcoat, long-skirted coat and frilled shirtbands. No doubt this was a good enough description of the appearance of one of the more prosperous farmers of the more advanced districts. The smaller farmer of the more remote and backward areas was quite different. He could easily be mistaken for a labourer. One old farmer cleric of Westmorland, born in 1719 who lived until 1812, was found by a visitor, sitting in his kitchen at the head of a large square table. He was dressed in a coarse blue frock trimmed with black horn buttons, a checked shirt, a leathern strap about his neck for a stock, a coarse apron and a pair of great wooden-soled shoes plated with iron to preserve them. With a child upon his knee, he was eating his breakfast. His wife and the rest of the children were some of them engaged in waiting upon the others, the rest in teasing and spinning wool, at which trade he was a great proficient. When this was ready for sale, it was packed in bundles of 16 lb. or 32 lb. weight. One or two of these bundles he carried upon his back and walked seven or eight miles to market, even in the depth of winter. His living was worth £43 a year, so he was £3 a year better off than the "Vicar of Wakefield".

The furniture of northern homes like this was heavy and rough, but eminently strong and serviceable. Almost everything was made of wood, pegs being used in place of nails. Wooden latches were fixed to doors and gates. Curiously carved arks and chests for storing oat cakes, malt, meal, preserves and dried meat were a great feature. Old china, pieces of flowered silk and satin dress material, the silver salt, a dozen plated apostle spoons, were all stored in one of these chests.

Bedsteads were grandiose in size and built of massive oak. Chairs were of wood, some of them being no more than the trunks of hollow trees, rudely adapted by the village carpenter or the home handy man, a species to which every man belonged.

Though not much different in dress and appearance from a prosperous labourer, of whom there were all too few, the small farmer was quite distinct from the worker. The social gap between these two classes became wider as the eighteenth century advanced, though many of the smaller farmers worked harder and lived no better than the farm servant.

In the early eighteenth century, long before John Ellman began to improve the Southdown sheep, the shepherd was an important man in Sussex and no doubt in other downland counties as well. He was decidedly the chief servant, and his calling was hereditary in his family. Shepherds worked on the same farm from generation to generation. A Sussex farmer would no more have thought of parting with his wife than his shepherd.

Then the Southdown farms were held in tenantry, i.e. in small scattered divisions, greater or less, and for the general benefit of all. The sheep, though owned by the different farmers, were herded in one flock, called the tenantry flock. One shepherd and his assistants managed the flock, and was paid by each of the owners in the ratio of his sheep to the whole number grazed. The shepherd had a personal interest in the flock. He had a money wage, and was also allowed to keep a certain number of sheep for his own profit. These tenantry flocks were often only wether flocks kept till three or four years old for until they attained that age they were scarcely considered mutton. This system of management was ancient, and was to be found so far away from Sussex as Wiltshire.

Like everybody else shepherds varied widely in character; and they developed individual idiosyncrasies owing to their lonely life, as L. P. Jacks showed much later in his book *Mad Shepherds*, 1923.

The shepherds of Salisbury Plain once had the reputation of being lazy in a very consistent way. If asked the way to some place when they were lying down beside their sheep, they would point with a leg rather than make the effort of getting up. One, indeed, when offered a shilling by a gentleman upon a horse said, "Thank ye kindly, sir, but will ye just get off your horse and slip it in my pocket."

Some of them were very different. One was greatly praised by Hannah More in her *Shepherd of Salisbury Plain*. David Saunders, a poor shepherd of West Lavington, and his father before him, herded sheep on the plain for at least a hundred years. David kept his Bible in the thatch of his hut and constantly read it. When, in 1771, he met Mr. Stedman, the new curate of the next village, David greeted him with an appropriate verse of scripture, "How beautiful upon the mountains are the feet of them that preach the gospel of peace, and bring glad tidings of good things." His profession has always been one that encouraged the contemplative life, and many stories have been told of shepherds' homely wisdom and caustic wit. It was a lonely life, and even men brought up to it sometimes felt that very keenly. A little poem, *The Shepherd and his Dog*, written by the Rev. William Lisle Bowles, who lived from 1762 to 1860, strikes this note plainly.

"My dog and I are both grown old;
On these wild downs we watch all day;
He looks in my face when the wind blows cold,
And this methinks I hear him say

The grey stone circle is below
The village smoke is at our feet;
We nothing hear but the sailing crow,
And wandering flocks that roam and bleat.

Far off the early horseman hies,
In shower and sunshine rushing on;
Yonder the dusty whirlwind flies
The distant coach is seen and gone."

Shepherds have always been the subject of song and story. The cowman, the wagoner, the ploughman have not been so greatly favoured so that there are few romantic or realistic literary descriptions of these men. Most of the people who wrote about them were concerned with their vices rather than their virtues. Poverty was always the result of sin or folly to eighteenth-century thinking, and, though the practical destitution of many of the farm workers was for them inescapable, it was not greatly pitied. It was more likely to be punished.

Already by 1775 Young could say that not one in a thousand of the cottagers had either land or cattle. He did not feel that this was any hardship because he believed correctly enough that the small holder worked harder and was less at his ease than the day labourer. Yet there were labourers who rose to be farmers. In Lancashire, for example, some were able to save enough to enter upon small farms, and afterwards, in proportion to the increase in their capitals, enter upon larger concerns. It was a hard and difficult road only to be traversed successfully by those of the most unremitting industry combined with the most penurious economy, and when all is said and done those who were able to overcome the difficulties and hardships and to achieve this meritorious ambition were few and far between. It was certainly easier or possibly easier in the Northern Counties, in Wales, in parts of Lincoln and in the extreme south-west, than it was in the counties along the south coast, in the Midlands and East Anglia, where it was for practical purposes almost if not quite impossible.

Some of these men were tremendously strong though few could have equalled the astonishing reaper of Great Doddington. In 1789 when he was eighty-eight years of age, this man undertook to reap a land of wheat sixty poles in length and seven yards in width. To the astonishment of everyone who saw him he performed the task with ease. He had about a mile to walk from home to his work, reaped the corn, and returned home again, "all in the space of thirteen hours".

On farms where turnips and clover were not yet grown, and they were still the majority at the end of the century, the day labourers spread muck, sowed the seed by hand broadcast, weeded the growing corn with spuds, just as they still do docking in the corn crops of East Suffolk today, dug and filled drains by hand, thatched the corn and haystacks, and wielded the flail in the threshing barn during the winter. If turnips were grown they had to be hoed several times, first bunched, then singled, and hoed again until the leaves had developed sufficiently to smother the weeds.

The farm servants, who lived in the farmhouse, were hired annually at the "statty" or Statute Fair. They might include a bailiff or foreman, a ploughman, cowman, shepherd, carter and dairymaids with some lads and lasses as helpers. Usually they were engaged for a year or less, often for six months. They received board, lodging and washing in the house and were paid a small yearly wage in addition. When looking for work they paraded in the good old-fashioned way with the insignia of their calling displayed in their hatbands or pinned to their coats.

At harvest many supplementary hands were necessary. The artisans and tradesmen of the towns helped. An extra supply of labour was the large bands of north-country people who came south, or Welshmen who travelled into the Midland and South-eastern Counties. Their own small harvests were later, and they could well afford to travel in order to earn some money before returning home to gather their own crops.

The need for these men was made more serious by the current prejudice against Sunday work. The seasons from 1776 were rather catchy and William Marshall, the great farming writer, who was then farming at Addiscombe, near Croydon, lost a good deal of hay and corn that might have been saved if his conscience and his men had allowed him to save it by working on Sundays. He was very troubled about it, but at last decided that he must save his harvest at the risk of breaking church and civil laws, and causing some unpleasantness with the men.

The first harvest he would have gathered in 1777 was spoiled by the weather. The hay lost its essence, and the corn became unwholesome, because he would not work on Sundays. Fearing the same consequences in later years he thought it reasonable to find out how his men spent the day first. The results of his inquiries were most inglorious. One man spent his day digging in his garden, another quarrelled with his neighbour, a third chose gambling as a recreation, a fourth, a scoffer and mocker at religion, spent Sunday blaspheming against his maker by way of amusing the hours of idleness. The rest of them were in the ale-house wasting their pitiful wages. Not unreasonably he thought they might have been just as harmlessly employed in saving the harvest.

So he began to work on Sundays, convinced it was the proper thing to do. The men were stimulated by double pay (2s. a day) and a substantial dinner of roast beef and plum pudding washed down by as much ale as it was fitting they should drink. This breakaway from tradition was severely censured by some of Marshall's neighbours, but he "eagerly wished to see it the common practice of his country; and was ambitious to set the patriotic example".

For moral support he appealed to no less a person than Dr. Johnson, who laid it down that an old law allowed the husbandman to work on Sundays at harvest. It declared that the Biblical exhortation, "Six days shalt thou labour, but in the seventh shalt thou rest; in earing time and in harvest shalt thou rest" was ceremonial, and only applied to the Jews of the Old Testament. Henry VIII had laid it down that it was right to work on Sundays if commanded by the Prince, or the Commonwealth, or in other time of necessity, "as for saving our corn and cattle when it is like to be in danger, or like to be destroyed, if remedy be not had in time."

The fate of the labourers remained very much in the hands of the local farmers who were still obliged to undertake the petty offices of churchwarden, way warden, overseers of the poor, constable and so on. Wages were low and there was much business connected with these offices.

There was a good deal of poaching, for sport by well-to-do and high-spirited young men, for profit or their own feeding by the workers who used this dangerous, severely punished method of adding to their scanty resources. Vagrants were numerous. They were hounded back to their own place at heavy cost and with tremendous effort, but conditions often forced the destitute and unemployed to take to the road. Orphan and bastard children were often apprenticed to farmers, when boys and girls alike had to do a great deal of heavy work for little reward. Some of them were treated well, of course, but in a harsh age these unprotected youngsters often suffered great hardships, occasionally real cruelty.

Starvation was never far from the door of the poor. Indeed people were known to die of it, and matters became worse with the rise of prices towards the end of the century. Four labourers were found dead of hunger and exposure in a field at Datchworth, Herts, about 1769, and in another place a labourer, his wife and two children were found dead in a house on the village green. These are recorded cases, and are unlikely to have been the only ones, for in bad seasons the price of corn rose to an impossible height. "In any parish where the officers responsible for poor relief were negligent or where there were no benevolent resident landlord willing to help cases of extreme suffering there was nothing to prevent the destitute from starving to death." This is very shocking to modern ideas, but it is undoubtedly correct.

When the revolutionary wars with France broke out in 1792 great progress had been made in farming technique. Over wide areas of the countryside the fields and farms had been rearranged, and new crops were being grown. Some new implements were already in use and new fertilizers were being suggested. Animal breeding had made great strides. Many farmers had made their fortunes, and the gulf between them and their workers had become quite unbridgeable. The wives of these men no longer wished to entertain the workers as lodgers in their homes, sharing the common meals in the farmhouse kitchen, so the living-in system disappeared in these districts. Elsewhere there was still a great deal of old-fashioned farm life, small farmers working side by side with the men and living in circumstances that were little different from those of cottagers; but gradually they, too, were infected with the passion for improvement, not to speak of better profits and greater incomes. There were great changes in fortune. Men who had been independent with their trivial rights of common, their acre or two of land, lost these things and became labourers. Some yeomen sold their freeholds and became tenant farmers, others became the leaders of the new industries. The less fortunate were caught in the fluctuations of prices and failed. The times were unsettled, often disastrous, but sometimes fortunate, and the changes that these conditions brought about were to become more marked in the following fifty years.

CHAPTER FIVE

The Farmer During the French Wars and After, 1793-1836

BETWEEN THE OUTBREAK of the French Wars in 1793 and the accession of Queen Victoria in 1837 farming prospered until the victory of Waterloo in 1815, and then sank into a depression that lasted two decades. The period of prosperity was marked by great advances in methods and productivity. Some farmers did very speculative ploughing out of marginal lands. They had to let this land revert to grass immediately the depression set in. It could hardly have been otherwise.

The first Board of Agriculture was established by Pitt in the same year as the war broke out, largely through the drive of enthusiasts like Sir John Sinclair, Bart., Arthur Young, and William Marshall, the last of whom claimed to have originated the idea. The Board was supported by Government funds. Other associations of landowners and farmers had been formed by private groups. The Bath and West of England Society was founded in 1777, the Highland and Agricultural Society in 1784, and many smaller and more local farming clubs, debating societies came into being. The Smithfield Club was founded in 1798.

All this was a sign of great activity amongst enlightened landlords and farmers, and was, of course, stimulated by the prospect of large profits in a time of rising prices. The lead already given by some owners of great agricultural estates was shared in by many others.

Of these the two best known are the Duke of Bedford and Coke of

H

Norfolk. Their annual sheep shearings were events of importance to agriculturists not only in this country, but all over Europe, and in far-away America.

Already Coke of Norfolk had improved the farming of his own estate. His great example had been followed by many Norfolk farmers, and by others in more distant places all over the country. He adopted and taught all the then recognized new principles. He marled and clayed the land, used a great deal of purchased manure, adopted the four-course rotation, grew wheat where only rye had been grown before, grew turnips, clover and sainfoin. By this means he was able to increase the number of livestock kept. His stall-fed cattle made quantities of rich manure from the oil cake and other nutritious feed he gave them. This rich manure produced heavy crops. Such visible and practical methods could not fail to impress his tenants. Farmers were eager to accept the leasehold farms that he had equipped with new houses, buildings and cottages.

The activities of the Board of Agriculture did not include an annual meeting and show. Its first project was an ambitious publishing enterprise, no less than a survey of the methods of the run of the cloth farmers as well as those of experimentalists and improvers in every county of the kingdom. The county reports the Board prepared were no doubt a useful record, but then, as now, the farmer was more easily convinced by what he could see than by what he could read about in learned books, or tomes that claimed to be learned.

Coke was one of the first to realize this. He organized his annual sheep shearing at Holkham, and showed improved animals and up-to-date implements. Upon the estate, too, his advanced theories could be seen in practice. A similar event was staged at Woburn Abbey by Francis, fifth Duke of Bedford.

The Holkham Sheep Shearing developed from homely discussions between Coke and his tenants. By 1819 when Coke was already an old man, he was considered the founder of a renowned system. His tenants were recognized as its leading exponents. In that year no less than five hundred guests dined in the state apartments as the guests of this great man. The Duke of Sussex was there, as were visitors from all parts of Europe. The conversation must have been animated in the extreme and doubtless ranged widely over multifarious aspects of farming.

The Duke of Bedford's Woburn Sheep Shearing was an equally elaborate affair. Some of the visitors arrived overnight, their only means of travel being on horseback or in horse-drawn conveyances. Early in the morning on the day there was most unusually heavy traffic on all the roads approaching the ground, not so thick as that approaching one of the great modern national shows like the "Royal" or the "Bath and West", but congested enough. Breakfast was eaten by the duke and his guests at 9 a.m., not a very early hour for those days, but early enough to be over before all the travellers had arrived. As soon as it was finished a great procession was formed to see the farm. The first objective was the yard where the shearers were at work. Here the visitors could see the tups that were to let on hire. The duke organized a competition for breeders of sheep and himself distributed prizes to the winners. In 1799 a Mr. Smith of Northampton gained one for a wether weighing 54 lb. a quarter. The Bedfordshire men won the awards for horse ploughing in that year, but Norfolk secured that for the best implement. When three o'clock came two hundred persons sat down in the abbey hall to a feast. Toasts and speeches lasted for three hours or more. The "Shearing" continued for five days.

Robert Salmon was surveyor to the Duke of Bedford for thirty years from 1790 to 1821. In his way he was as distinguished as his noble employer. He was one of those men of many and varied interests, well described as a universal genius, who could only flourish before the days when knowledge became so narrowly departmentalized. He was responsible for designing the duke's Home Farm and estate buildings, models for their time, and his powers of invention were directed at a number of widely diversified objects. Naturally many of these were agricultural. These included a chaff-cutting machine, a drill, an improved plough, a "scuffler" or cultivator, a self-raking reaping machine of a type that only came into use a half a century later, and a threshing machine that was similarly unnoticed at the time. A hay-making machine was another thing. Besides these he gained awards from the Society of Arts for surgical instruments, a canal lock, apparatus for pruning trees, a mantrap, and earth walls, truly a man of extraordinary ability.

Under such a surveyor the Duke of Bedford's estates could only have been well managed. It was not always so. Far away in Cumberland John Christian Curwen, one of the largest colliery owners in that county, found that his farm was losing money, because he had left the management entirely in the hands of a bailiff. This disconcerted him extremely. Though he had little or no experience he decided to run the farm himself.

It was not long before he started the Workington Agricultural Society and held an annual meeting at his Schoose Farm. Soon this meeting almost equalled those at Holkham and Woburn. At the first in 1805 some 460 people dined at Curwen's expense either in tents or in a wooden booth. A few years later the gathering was said, with what exactness it is not possible to decide, to have become the largest provincial meeting of farmers in England. All the agricultural celebrities attended, the Dukes of Norfolk and Bedford, Coke, and Sinclair amongst them. The proceedings ended with a ball given by Mrs. Curwen in the Assembly Rooms at Workington on the evening of the second day.

These individual organizers of early agricultural shows were all great landowners. The greatest of them all was the King, and he, no less than they, was an enthusiast for the new farming. His reclamation work in Windsor Great Park is well known. Out of this waste, as it was when he took it in hand, he created the Norfolk and Flemish farms, and made them examples of the two most approved systems of agriculture of that age. George III was a great believer in oxen for ploughing. To prove he was right he once arranged a ploughing match at Windsor between his own ploughs and a double-furrow plough invented by Lord John Somerville, one-time president of the Board of Agriculture. Another of his activities was the importation of Merino sheep from Spain, for which he employed the services of Sir Joseph Banks.

Royalty, the ducal houses, the ranks of the great landowning nobility, all set the example of new and improved systems of arable farming and breeding and feeding livestock to the ordinary farmers, their tenants and neighbours. Many learned from the experiments made, often at financial loss that made the farmer working for his living doubtful of their value. Others kept on the even tenor of their way doings things mainly as their fathers had before them. Even they were not completely impervious to the new methods, but were quite prepared to adopt them when convinced that they were profitable.

One such was Wilby Goodheart, described by Surtees. He was one of the old-fashioned tarry-at-home school of farmers, neat, careful, prudent, honest. He had been on the same estate for sixty years, and was the sort of man called upon to give evidence to one or other of the Select Committees on distress in agriculture that collected such masses of evidence between 1820 and 1836 with no very tangible result. Goodheart's little farm was a perfect model of neatness and productiveness.

His ordinary dress was a straight-cut, single-breasted, large-buttoned blue coat on the straight collar of which his own grey hair fell in curly locks. On Sundays he wore a pair of sky-blue stockings and square-toed shoes with silver buckles, all in the fashion of a bygone day. He seldom went from home except to church and did not frequent markets, losing time on his farm and money at the ordinary. He sold his corn to the miller, his neighbour. His daughter carried his butter and eggs to the village shop at Hillingdon. The shop supplied his own wants.

He was one of the draining, manuring, hard-working breed of farmers. His stay-at-home habits did not prevent him from carrying out small but continuous improvements. He always had some little job of this kind in hand or in prospect, a hedge to make straight, some land to lay better away, some pit to fill up and make level ground for cropping, or some gate to move to a more convenient position. Goodheart was the ideal of a man, not given to flights of fancy, or speculative interest in every novelty, but one who did the land well as his principles demanded, and left his farm in better case than he entered it.

Genial though they might be in family relations and friendship, farmers of this type had nothing but contempt for their less conscientious fellows. Martin Poyser could carry a very contemptuous expression in his black eyes set in a ruddy face, if at market he happened to meet a farmer whose methods he did not approve of. Poyser's particular delight was to criticize every action of Luke Britton "whose fallows were not well cleaned, who didn't know the rudiments of hedging and ditching, and showed but a small share of judgement in the purchase of winter stock". Luke Britton could not make a remark, even upon the weather, but Martin Poyser detected in it a taint of that unsoundness and general ignorance which was palpable in all his farming operations.

Poyser lived in the Hall Farm, where the front gate was never opened. Long grass and great hemlocks grew close against it. The former great days before the place had degenerated from The Hall, the home of a country squire, into the Hall Farm, were most obviously ended. The life of The Hall had changed its focus, and no longer radiated from the parlour, but from the kitchen, and the farmyard. Numerous as such changes were a hundred and fifty years ago they are more numerous now, though the parlours of our richer farmers today are often furnished with expensive and shrewdly collected period pieces. They are very different from Martin's. In his home the former dining-room, with its large open fireplace and rusty iron firedogs, displayed only the bare boards of its floor. At the far end fleeces of wool were stacked, and some empty corn bags occupied the middle. The parlour contained several clothes' horses, a pillion, a spinning wheel and an old box wide open, stuffed full of coloured rags. An old wooden doll, much damaged by too loving use and quite noseless, rested on the edge of the box. Beside it was a little chair, and the butt end of a boy's leather long-lashed whip. Just two lumber rooms in fact.

An old ballad praises the life that was led in such farmhouses as these. *The Farmer's Son* sings dolefully of the good old days as every generation has always done.

"When my mother she was knitting, my sister she would spin,
And by their good industry they kept us neat and clean;
I rose up in the morning, with my father went to plough
How happily we lived then to what we do now!

Then to market with the fleece when the little herd was shorn,
And our neighbours we supplied with a quantity of corn,
For half a crown a bushel we would sell it then I vow.
How happily we lived then to what we do now!

How merrily would the farmers then sing along the road,
When wheat was sold at market for five pounds a load;
They'd drop into an ale-house and drink 'God speed the plough'.
How happily we lived then to what we do now!"

Miss Mary Mitford, writing between 1824 and 1832, a period truly "bad times for farmers", looked back ten or twelve years to a time when she often used to visit a prosperous farmer at Three Mile Cross, near Reading. The approach to his farmhouse was along a lane through "a solid suburb of ricks of all sorts, shapes and dimensions. Then came the farm like a town; a magnificent series of buildings, stables, cart houses, cow houses, graneries and barns, that might hold all the corn of the parish, placed at all angles to each other, and mixed with smaller habitations for pigs, dogs and poultry." The old substantial farm-house looked out over all.

Large establishments like this flourished all across the Berkshire and Wiltshire downs, were scattered through the Midlands, were numerous in East Anglia, the newly created border county of North-umberland and the Lowlands of Scotland. Many of them are still to be seen.

"The master of this land of plenty was well fitted to preside over it; a thick stout man of middle height, and middle aged, with healthy ruddy square face, all alive with intelligence and good humour." This man was able to manage his own farm and two stewardships as well. Frequent arbitrations were put to him by both parties to a dispute. In addition "he was a sort of standing overseer and churchwarden; he ruled his own hamlet like a despotic monarch, and took a prime minister's share in the government of the large parish to which it was attached". He was, indeed, a shining example of the centuries old succession of great yeomen farmers who had accepted all these responsi-bilities cheerfully, and whose successors still do so.

Though he must have been extremely busy his life was not only devoted to work. "He had always leisure to receive his friends at home, or to visit them abroad; to take journeys to London, or make excursions to the seaside (in this, at least, he must have been exceptional). His great amusement was coursing. He kept several brace of capital greyhounds."

His wife played an active part in the economy of the household, and altogether the family formed an example of the best kind of large-scale farm management at that time.

The practical part of the work was as well done as the appearance of the property and its proprietor suggested. In May gangs of men and women were to be seen in the large wheatfields hoeing out the weeds, as many as fourteen in one gang. For haymaking and harvest all the locals who could be induced to join in the work were collected. The village shoemaker, the wheelwright, the publican, his two pretty daughters, and a visitor from London were all recruited.

This great farmer would probably only have snorted could he have seen one of his contemporaries who lived near Weyhill at his ploughing. Perhaps he did when he went to the sheep fair at that place. Who knows now? The Weyhill man did his ploughing with asses. He had two teams of these useful animals, and penned them on his fallows at night like sheep. In the winter he foddered them in the yard? A similar ploughing team was used at about this time by some of the small farmers in Worcestershire.

In 1812 wheat sold at the famine price of 126s. 6d. a quarter at a time when the labourers' wages was 1s. 6d. a day, paid only for the days he worked. There was no guaranteed week then. This high price was exceptional, but in spite of great fluctuations prices during the wars were generally high enough to make the corn-growing farmers prosperous. In the Midlands as in Berkshire great corn stacks stood in the rick yards. The homesteads were occupied by rich farmers who could afford to keep their corn till prices had risen. They rode to market on well-groomed horses, or weighing down one side of a gig. "They probably thought of the coach with some contempt, as an accommodation for people who had not their own gigs, or who, wanting to travel to London or such distant places, belonged to the trading and less solid part of the nation."

But farmers of wide acres were and still are in a minority in our countryside. Every farm was by no means the scene of such earnest and active up-to-date neatness. The arable Midlands still clung very largely to fallow instead of adopting the new crops. Here one innovating farmer talked of Sir Humphrey Davy having fairly been driven out of a parish by popular dislike.

The prosperity and position of the hereditary yeoman farmer was acceptable to all, but the new rich of the time were very generally condemned for aping the manners of the gentry. They were condemned as middle-class upstarts who wished to rank with gentlemen, and thought they might do so by wearing kid gloves and buying new furniture—a foible that human nature has not yet overcome. A popular catch ran:

> "Man, Tallyho!
> Miss, Piano,
> Wife, Silk and Satin,
> Boy, Greek and Latin,
> And you'll all be gazetted."

Or in other words go bankrupt. It became particularly popular when prices fell after peace was declared, the farmers being accused of wasting their money on unaccustomed, silly and unnecessary luxuries when they had it, instead of saving it for use in a.bad time. They ought to have kept to their former simple and industrious habits:

> "Man to the Plough,
> Wife to the Cow,
> Girl to the Yarn,
> And your rent will be netted."

Such accusations have always been made against any class of men who have been caught unawares in a time of falling prices and depression. Much worse difficulties had to be overcome if an estate had been neglected or badly managed, where necessary repairs had not been done and draining on heavy clay land neglected. Farms on such estates, and doubtless there were more than that described by George Eliot in *Felix Holt*, were held by men who had begged hard to succeed their fathers in getting poorer, where the highest rate of increase was in the arrears of rent, and where the master in crushed hat and corduroys, looked pitiably lean and careworn by the side of the pauper labourers. These men did not know which way to turn. They were still more hard put to it if they left their farms. Many of them did so, "with a waggon full of furniture and utensils, a file of receipts, a wife with five children, and a shepherd dog in low spirits".

The most shocking effects of the sudden and unprecedented fall in prices were reported to the Board of Agriculture in the early months of 1816. Corn and cattle had to be sold at whatever prices they would fetch, the byres and yards were not restocked, rents failed to be paid, and bankruptcies were much more numerous than usual. Country tradesmen found it more than usually difficult to collect their bills if they could get paid at all. Some farmers packed up their furniture and chattels in their wagons and drove their livestock off by night. Others paid their Ladyday rent. Then between harvest and Michaelmas they sold off everything and vanished. How many did this it is difficult to estimate. Probably only a few despite the general distress. Those who did would be remarkable at any time and their number likely to be exaggerated.

Some counties were not so badly affected as others, particularly where, as in Kent, the hop crop helped to save the situation, or in the grassland counties where hard-working families worked small farms, often mainly grassland. On such farms outgoings were small and, though incomings were not large, there was usually some small thing to take to market every week, pounds of butter, baskets of eggs and poultry, fruit and so on.

In the prosperous years no doubt the rich farmers on the larger holdings went in for unaccustomed luxuries. Who does not in the optimistic belief that the good times will last forever? Their prosperity was apparent in their appearance. One foreign tourist travelling from Dover to London was greatly impressed by the neatness of the hedges and thought that the farmhouses looked so clean and tidy that they might just have been built. To his surprise one of his fellow travellers who descended from the coach at an intermediate stage was greeted by a wife and four daughters all dressed in white muslin. They all looked so fashionable that he asked who the lady and gentleman were. The coachman dismissed his inquiry summarily with the curt reply, "A farmer and his wife."

The home life of that class of farmer was doubtless distinguished by the refinement described by Mary Mitford and others. Visitors would be offered a drink of sherry wine instead of the vulgar home brew of former days, a habit that ran on all fours with the hunting and the piano. George Borrow, that lover of old England, despised such habits. Sherry was for him incomparably less heartening than bright home-brew. The food on the tables of these men, too, was probably more like that of the gentry than of the majority of lesser farmers.

All over the country average farmers ate pig meat as their most usual flesh food just as the labourers did. The difference was that the men ate bacon or pork less frequently, possibly once a week. Unfortunately there is little tangible and exact evidence. The poverty of the labourers was such that a good many philanthropists and others collected details of their budgets, but the farmer's plate was not inquired into very carefully. He was presumed to be well enough.

About 1808 the middle-class farmers in Cheshire seldom indulged themselves with much fresh animal food. After a market they might buy a piece of cheap meat to last a few days. For the rest of the week a little bacon or beef of their own curing gave a relish to their large dish of potatoes or cabbage. Whey or buttermilk from the dairy completed the meal.

Potatoes were a comparatively new crop, but were fairly generally eaten in a good many counties. Lancashire, with its large manufacturing population, grew and ate a great many. From Derby northwards oat bread or haver cake was usual. It was made by the sour-dough method. Bread was made of maslin in Durham, and many potatoes were grown. Not so much rye as formerly was grown in Northumberland, but a good deal of maslin bread was, nevertheless, still eaten. The famed "statesmen", small occupier-owners, of Cumberland made their bread of barley or a mixture of barley and rye. Oatcake was made, and oatmeal made into hasty pudding with butter, treacle, milk or beer served for breakfast, and often supper. Potatoes eaten with a little butter or cream for sauce had recently become a main article in the diet. Few families dined without them in 1797. Though the farmers of Westmorland rarely ate butcher meat fifty years before, their habits had changed. Pottage with a little cheese was breakfast, butcher meat with potatoes or pudding dinner, and potatoes or pottage and bread and cheese supper. Clap bread or girdle cakes was usual. Dorothy Wordsworth dined at a public house on porridge with a second course of Christmas pies in 1801, and at Grisdale on ham and bread and milk in 1802.

Nottingham, Stafford, Oxford, Salop, Worcester, Essex, Dorset, Devon, Wiltshire and Cornwall are counties where potatoes formed a new and helpful addition to the diet, more particularly of the poorer people. The farmers in Leicestershire ate their own produce in 1809, as no doubt they had long since done. Their tables were supplied with wheaten bread, beef, mutton, cheese and butter of the best. The same conditions were found in Rutland though some people ate barley bread or bread made of barley and wheat mixed.

All over the south-west barley was the bread corn of the poorer people, though it may not have been the only bread corn eaten. Charles Vancouver discovered in 1808 that barley constituted a very large proportion of the bread corn used in Devonshire farmhouses. On the moorlands barley bread and potatoes formed a large part of the food of the population, but they also used wheat broth seasoned with a small piece of meat and pot-herbs, and for variety pies made of bacon and potatoes, like those known as shepherd's pie. Pea broth seasoned with bacon was another farmhouse dish in this county, and near the coast an occasional dish of fish made a welcome change. On this diet the Devon men were famous for their strength and hardihood.

The simplicity of their diet shows that the majority of farmers were living and working in the simple manner of their ancestors. Comparatively few of them were numbered amongst the rich and famous men who were criticized for their snobbish attempts to live up to the standards and to follow the fashions of the leisure class.

The debacle after Waterloo affected them all. Prosperity vanished like the smoke of last night's fire, or as Lady Dorothy Neville once said "Fortunes made in no time are like shirts made in no time; it's ten to one if they hang together." Almost every farmer was affected, some, of course, more than others; all landowners, too, but good management did not disappear at a stroke. William Cobbett, who began his *Rural Rides* in the early years of the depression, was still able to discover and commend good farmers. His contempt for bad ones was unmeasured.

Cobbett was himself a good farmer though he spent a good deal of time absent from his holding. For two years he was in prison. Later he rode all over the country inquiring into rural conditions. He bought a house at Botley, in Hampshire, situated on a creek of the River Hamble, and Fairthorne Farm, comprising some 300 acres, in the same neighbourhood. Here he lived well according to his own modest ideas. He dispensed fine hospitality to his friends, kept a kennel of greyhounds for coursing as well as other hounds, and made himself a local name in garden management, growing famous fruit, vegetables and flowers, and demonstrating in a practical way, the culture of water-melons, Carolina beans and Indian corn, three things for which he had a foible.

When Cobbett set out on his first farming tour in October, 1821 he was extremely well qualified for the job, much more so than Arthur Young when he made his *Six Weeks Tour* in 1767. Already in 1821 the state of agriculture was the concern of Government, and Select Committees of the House of Commons had spent a great deal of time in collecting evidence about rural distress. Having collected it they printed it, but there does not seem to have been any other tangible result.

The winter of 1821 found Cobbett in Suffolk and Norfolk. Between Bury St. Edmunds and Norwich the farming was praiseworthy despite the difficult times. The land was clean and everything done in a

58. DINGLE'S HAND-DIBBLING MACHINE IN OPERATION. *Farmer's Magazine*, March, 1846. The worker's garb is noteworthy

59. Steam engine, portable, driving a threshing machine. From *Farmer's Magazine*, Vol. 12, 1845

60. MR. JONAS WEBB of Brabraham, Cambridge. A great breeder of Southdown sheep. From *Farmer's Magazine,* March, 1845

61. COLEMAN'S PATENT EXPANDING LEVER HARROW. From *Farmer's Magazine*, February, 1846

62. (*top*): Ploughing. (*bottom*): Harrowing. Both from pencil sketches by G.S.L. *circa* 1849 in a scrap-book of that date in the author's possession

63. (*top*): MAKING HAY. (*bottom*): MOWING GRASS. Pencil sketches by
G.S.L. *circa* 1849. From the scrap-book

64. Loading the hay wagon. A pencil sketch by G.S.L. about 1849. From the scrap-book.

65. A VICTORIAN FARMYARD. A pencil sketch by G.S.L., 1849. From the scrap-book

66. SPRING PLOUGHING. The morning halt for a snack. From
William Howitt's *Book of the Seasons*, 9th ed., 1851

67. WINTER WORK. Threshing with the flail. From William Howitt's
Book of the Seasons, 9th ed., 1851

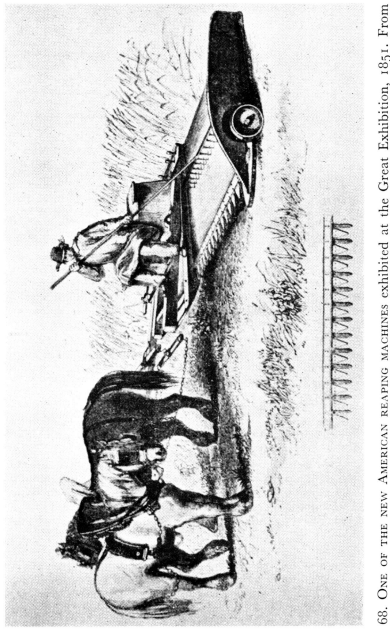

68. One of the new American reaping machines exhibited at the Great Exhibition, 1851. From Journal R.A.S.E., 1851

69. RABBIT SHOOTING. From an illustration in Ward Lock's *Farm
Management* (no date)—about a century old

70. A FARM WORKER and his cottage of cob and thatch—an old-style bungalow. From F. G. Heath, *The English Peasantry*, 1874

71. MAKING STRAW ROPES. From L. G. Seguin, *Rural England*, 1885

72. The shepherd's Christmas Day. From a colour print of the early Victorian age in the author's collection

73. A NINETEENTH-CENTURY FARMHAND, MOWING. From a water-colour in the author's possession

masterly manner, Cobbett saw an occasional crop of rape and several of swedes. Rents, however, had to be reduced. Cobbett acknowledged the respect in which Coke was held, but did not agree with his politics as might have been expected. He returned home carrying with him the weightless burden of "great admiration and respect for, this county of excellent farmers, and hearty, open, and spirited men". A little later he admired the management of some enclosed fields near Royston, though no Swedish turnips were grown and the crops were not drilled. It is a pity he was not more particular in his description of the men who were doing the work.

Though he found much to admire on the large farms along the Wiltshire Avon between Marlborough and Salisbury he is equally neglectful of the persons responsible. In August 1826 the stackyards there were full of "banging" wheat ricks, five to fifteen in each, besides barley ricks and hay ricks. In a piece of wheat stubble, 400 acres all in one field, he saw a sheep fold of one acre containing about 4,000 sheep and lambs. At one farm between Pewsey and Upavon, he counted more than 300 hogs in one stubble. The sheep fold was the main source of manure thereabouts. It "was certainly the most delightful farming in the world". At other times Cobbett found excellent farming in such widely separated places as Herefordshire, Lincoln and Northumberland.

Production continued as it must do if the individual farming enterprise is not to cease. The continuing years of low, almost unremunerative prices, could only be combated by more intensive work. Many farmers devoted themselves to this object. The great livestock breeders of the eighteenth century found worthy successors in the early nineteenth. Charles and Robert Colling, Thomas Bates of Kirklevington, the Booths and Sir Charles Knightley became famous as breeders of Shorthorns. The Herefords were improved by Benjamin Tomkins, John Hewer and the Prices. The Devons became a hobby of Francis Quartly with whom the Davys competed. Coke of Norfolk favoured this breed. Many flockmasters in different parts of the country followed Ellman's example, and other breeds besides the New Leicester and Southdown came into prominence in suitable localities.

The large arable farms that had been cut out of the waste of Lincoln Heath, the Wolds of the East Riding, the Northumbrian Hills, grew crops that were almost weedless and highly productive by the standards of the time. New and improved ploughs had been designed to assist the work. The seed drill was gradually becoming usual and other mechanical aids were being developed. John Grey of Dilston was working in Northumberland, Smith of Deanston was developing and publicizing his system of "thorough drainage and subsoil ploughing" for reclaiming heavy wet land. New manures like Chilean nitrate of soda and Peruvian guano were beginning to be discussed. Bones and bone dust had become popular for the restoration of exhausted pastures. All this was the spring foretelling the summer that was to come in the first four decades of the reign of Queen Victoria.

This was one aspect of farming just before 1837. It was the best practice and cannot have been general. The average did not at all compare with it. Winter feed was still short on many farms where the cattle half starved through the bitter winter months in insanitary and ruinous shacks that did not deserve the name of buildings. Many farmers used old-fashioned implements which often appeared less practical than they were in fact. Most of the work was done by hand. The seed was sown broadcast from a bag slung over the sower's shoulder. Manure was carted from the yards and spread with a fork. The growing crops were hoed by hand on the best farms, but many farmers left their crops to struggle for existence against the weeds without any help. The harvest was won manually. Hay was cut with the scythe, corn with the sickle. The grain was threshed out of the ear with the flail. Machinery was as yet almost unknown on most farms.

The farmers who worked in this old-fashioned way were like Johnny Wopstraw. He sat down to his twelve o'clock dinner of potatoes and bacon and gooseberry pudding with his wife, children and servants. This was a fine old-fashioned traditional scene, but new ideas were gradually changing it. Instead of the family and the servants sitting together at one huge rectangular table, the farmer and his family had begun to make a distinction between themselves and the servants. They all ate together in the large farmhouse kitchen, but the family sat at a table covered with a spotless cloth. A little apart the single men and maids sat on benches and stools at another table, the bare board scrubbed to a whiteness equalling the cloth. Maids and men shared the ample family fare. Small beer and cider was the usual drink, but tea was becoming popular with the ladies of the family. The servants' meals were seasoned with bucolic flirtation and rustic romance.

Childhood and youth were the happiest time in many a farm servant's life. Then he or she was living in a farmhouse. The farm worker, who lived in, was sure of good food, the same as that his employer ate. If not very varied in composition, there was rude plenty and amply sufficient for all. The men slept in a loft, usually shared with his fellows, but a crowded bedroom was a commonplace to him from boyhood, and he did not feel the lack of privacy. His meagre annual wage paid for his clothes, and provided a little pocket money to spend at the fair, the wake, Easter and Christmas.

When he married and went to live in a cottage he found things very different. Wages, that had never been sufficient to provide for a family, were slowly rising, but not fast enough to meet the rise in prices. There was great suffering and great discontent. The men could not understand why they should be so poor. Many well-to-do philanthropists tried to help them by suggesting economies that the men might practise so as to reduce their cost of living. Different and cheaper kinds of food did not appeal to men used to bread and cheese, and a bit of bacon at the weekend.

When there was a bad harvest, the workers starved. In 1795 the price of wheat rose to 104s. a quarter, a price that meant the labourers went hungry. It was in this year that Mr. Whitbread made the first attempt to introduce legal minimum wages, but his bill did not become law.

Something had to be done. The magistrates at Speenhamland in Berkshire invented a system of allowances. They laid it down that when a gallon loaf of second-grade flour weighing 8 lb. 11 oz. cost 1s. a man must have 3s. a week for himself and 1s. 6d. for his wife and each of his children. When the loaf was 1s. 4d. the man was to have 4s. and his wife and children each 1s. 10d. This provided the man with three gallon loaves a week, and his wife and children one and a half each, a standard of living that was not very generous.

When the men could not get full-time employment with one farmer, they were shared out among the ratepayers, or else their labour was sold by the parish to employers at a low rate to ensure some work. The parish contributed what was necessary to bring the labourer's wage up to the scale of the rates. This system did no more and no less than create a race of paupers, though some few must have been able to keep their heads above water. These few were a tiny minority.

For most of the workers, life held out no hope of ever rising out of the morass in which they were sunk.

The system spread all over the country, and lasted for forty years. A generation grew up that never knew what it was to earn enough money to be independent of poor relief. The extra money from the rates they looked upon as a right, and called it their "allowance".

Meanwhile the war went on. Scarcity prices ruled. Only in six of the twenty-two years between 1793 and 1814 was an average harvest gathered. The crops failed disastrously in seven years, 1795, 1799, 1800, and from 1809 to 1814 inclusive. Though more land was down to corn than ever before, the supply was not large enough to feed the people, and death from starvation was not uncommon.

The mens' condition did not improve when the wars ended. The trade depression that followed forced the farmers to look to machines to save labour, and to new crops and fertilizers to increase yields. Only measures of this kind were drastic enough to enable them to keep solvent. Many failed to do so.

The most labour-saving machine that had so far been invented was the threshing machine, and it was a famous economizer. Threshing had been a job that kept the men busy in the barn all the winter. With a machine the work could be done much more quickly, and at times when the farmer wanted to sell his wheat and barley, or to use it. Advantageous as it was to the farmer, the threshing machine was very disadvantageous to the men. They saw that it meant the loss of much of their winter work, and that they would be worse off than ever.

Almost intolerable conditions amongst the men had led to rioting in 1795 and in 1816. These riots were suppressed, but discontent natural enough in all conscience, though misguided, stirred the men up to worse violence in 1830. The disturbances began in Kent, and rapidly spread through the south-west. Workhouses were destroyed at Selbourne and Headley; ricks were burned down at many places. Large bands of workers called at farms, and demanded that the machines should be destroyed. They asked for money, too. They had very real grievances. They lived in the depths of poverty, and they saw another part of their employment imperilled. Even in the harvest their living was uncertain. Four harvest workers were found dead of starvation under a hedge in the same year. The country was terrified of revolution, and the ruling class crushed the "rebels" quite ruthlessly. Hundreds of labourers were put in prison. Many were sentenced to death, or to transportation for life, and those who escaped imprisonment sank once more into the apathy of despair.

The Reform Act was passed in 1832, but this did not affect the farm worker at all. The New Poor Law passed in 1834 did. It abolished outdoor relief to the able-bodied. Almost immediately the farmers began to find that they could employ more full-time labour; but the wages paid were starvation wages. In Dorset some labourers were told that their miserable pittance of 9s. a week was to be reduced to 8s. and then to 7s. A threat was made to reduce it still further to 6s. It would have been impossible for the men to buy bread for their families for such a small sum. Two of the men, George Loveless and his brother, tried to form a trade union to put themselves into a better position to fight against these reductions. They were told it was illegal to form such a union, and were arrested. After a long trial they were sentenced to transportation for life. The whole country became very indignant at this severity, and their sentence was reduced. After some years the survivers were allowed to return to their homes. These men were the renowned "Tolpuddle Martyrs".

Only the barest outline of the general condition of the labourer during the period is given here, because the story has been told fairly often, and should be pretty well known. It is obvious that only by the most savage and exacting fortitude and frugality could a labourer save a little money, or rise in the social scale. There were, of course, foremen's jobs and bailiffs' jobs, better paid than the average. Indeed, farm workers were classified as bailiffs, ploughmen, shepherds and labourers, by J. C. Loudon. He added female servants and apprentices, though the last were unusual except in the west of England, where some parishes put out pauper children, both boys and girls, as apprentices to farmers.

A bailiff was only necessary on the largest farms where the master was largely occupied in management and required someone to oversee the detailed everyday work. Young men who took these positions were usually of some education, and used the job as a stepping stone to gain experience for a position as a gentleman's bailiff or land steward. The most that an ordinary farmer required for this purpose was a head ploughman, who worked the best team, took the lead, and set an example to the other ploughmen in every description of work.

Loudon thought it best to employ the ordinary ploughmen on a yearly contract and to have them live in, but this was impossible if the men were married. In that event cottages ought to be provided for them. He did not approve of employing weekly or occasional ploughmen. They were uncertain of their employment, and this made them unreliable. Besides that they had no loyalty to any one employer, as they were continually wandering from one master to another, who might, though in all the circumstances it seems unlikely, bid against one another for the man's services at a busy time. A man who had a family, he cogently remarks, was more reliable because his domestic responsibilities tied him down to regular industry.

Hiring servants at the "statty" or Statute Fair was beginning to fall into disrepute. It enabled men to get a job without a character, so much had the traditional safeguards fallen into disuse, promoted dissipation, and caused a cessation of country business for some days, after which work was only slowly and reluctantly resumed. The common perquisites of ale and cider were very bad. "Nothing could be more absurd than permitting a ploughman to stop for half an hour on a winter's day to drink ale, while his horses are neglected and shivering with cold."

Besides ploughmen a few labourers were necessary on every farm of any size. A man who could hedge and ditch, clean out furrows, keep up the garden, maintain the farm roads, and do other odd jobs never lacked employment on a well-maintained farm. Another man was essential for caring for the livestock, looking after the cattle, pigs and straw yard, and killing pigs and sheep when required. These would be able to help in hay-time, harvest, threshing, and carting and spreading dung, but none of them should be casual labour hired by the day.

The problem of how to dispose of the numerous fatherless orphans and bastards was one that puzzled many of the Guardians. An easy method was discovered by the authorities in Devonshire and other parts of the south-west. The children of paupers as well as the orphans were put out at the tender age of seven or eight years old, as apprentices to farmers, bound until they were twenty-one years of age. The only condition was that the farmer should provide them with "every necessity", but there was no system of inspection, so that the children's necessities were often very economically provided.

William Marshall thought these apprentices were fortunate because the farmers provided them with better sustenance than they could expect to receive from their parents. Moreover, the children were inured to labour and industry, and in the end very profitable employees. He was disappointed to discover that the system did not work out in this way. Instead of treating their apprentices as their adopted children or relations, the farmers often kept them in a state of the most abject drudgery. The consequence was that as soon as they were old enough to earn their own living the apprentices went off. Local papers were full of advertisements for the apprehension of runaway apprentices. If the masters were kindly in their treatment the children often grew up "to become most valuable members of the community". A more natural seminary of working husbandmen could hardly be devised, and Marshall thought that with proper safeguards it might usefully be extended to other districts.

When they grew up, apprentices, like other rural children, might become specialists in any of the numerous farm jobs, or might be general labourers. The class of worker upon whom Loudon placed the most value was the shepherd. He must be the most steady and attentive type, and should be well paid and comfortably treated if only for reasons of self-interest. In lambing time, for example, much of the farmer's property was in the shepherd's hands, and its protection depended upon his unwearied exertion early and late.

The shepherd was a busy man at lambing, and at washing and shearing. At other seasons he had to watch over his sheep with paternal care, to see that they did not suffer from foot rot in damp places, to protect them from natural enemies, and generally to treat them for the diseases to which they were prone. To an outside observer he might seem slow and idle, but in those moments of most apparent idleness he was watching carefully for anything that might go amiss. His boy, if he had one, had less responsibility and might dream away a summer day in indolence, as vacant minded as he has sometimes been described,

> "There was a shepherd boy
> Stretching his lazy limbs on the rough straw
> In vacant happiness. A tattered sack
> Covered his sturdy loins, while his rude legs
> Were decked with uncouth patches of all hues,
> Iris and jet, through which his sunburnt skin
> Peep'd forth in dainty contrast. He was a glory

For painter's eye . . . his indolent gaze
Reck'd not of natural beauties; his delights
Were gross and sensual . . . he went plodding on
His long accustomed path; and when his cares
Of daily duties were o'erpass'd, he ate,
And laughed and slept with a most drowsy mind."

In districts where large flocks were kept along the chalk downs in the south from Wiltshire to Sussex, and in the Romney Marsh, and in the hills of the north, sheep washing was a time of immense activity. The wild hills of the north were lonelier and more desolate than the southern downlands, and the sheep had to be collected from greater distances. At dawn the work began. All the shepherds of the district, each accompanied by a couple of dogs, co-operated. They gathered the sheep and drove them to the usual washing place. All the neighbours assembled to help or look on. Everybody joined in a repast, and then the washers got ready for their most arduous job.

The washing place was a pool of three feet or so deep. The sheep were drifted out of the fold through a narrow outlet. Two or three active workers caught them one by one and threw them into the water in succession as fast as the washers could deal with them. The sheep resisted, and a good deal of muscular effort was necessary to overpower them. The washer laid hold of his victim, turned the sheep on to its back in the water, and, after a little rubbing of the wool, turned it back upwards. He then compressed the wool by grasping it between his hands and squeezed most of the grease and filth out of the fleece. It sounds a longish job, but in reality took only a few moments. An expert washer could cleanse about a hundred sheep an hour. The water was usually very cold, and the washers did their best to keep up their own bodily heat by large potations of hot ale and spirits and water. Their precautions sometimes overcame them. When all the sheep were done another general repast was eaten, no doubt with a display of high spirits at the completion of a none-too-pleasant task.

The shepherd was slightly better paid than the general run of farm workers, and was sometimes allowed to keep a sheep or two of his own with his master's flock. Occasionally part of his wages were paid in lambs. His condition of employment and frequent spells of work away from the village helped him to save a little money, if he was determined to do so. He had opportunities that did not exist for the other men, but they were nearly as exiguous. The most stringent self-denial, a doing without things that were not absolute necessities, had to be exercised by any farm employee who was at.all ambitious.

One Sussex shepherd, John Dudeney, who was born at Rottingdean in 1782, is an example of what could be done in spite of the tremendous obstacles that confronted a man of his class at that time. His parents taught him to read and write and a little arithmetic, but his education did not last very long. At eight years old he helped with the sheep, and sometimes drove the plough team.

Dudeney's early training had given him a taste for reading, and he spent his minute wages in buying books at Lewes Fair. He was allowed the keeping of one sheep for himself, the lamb and wool of which brought in about fifteen shillings a year. This money he saved to buy a watch. Trapping wheatears, then a table delicacy in London, added a few shillings to his earnings.

As he grew older he changed his master from time to time, but remained a shepherd and continued his miscellaneous reading, miscellaneous because he had to read the books he could get hold of. In time he became a head shepherd at Rottingdean. He went on snaring wheatears, and in the season caught as many as thirteen dozen in a day. These he sold to a Brighton caterer at 1s. 6d. a dozen, thus earning a fabulous sum. At this place he had more opportunities for study. He was helped by the vicar and by his aunt. He even studied the Hebrew scriptures in the original. At length in 1804 he gave up shepherding, and opened a school at Lewes.

In Suffolk another ploughboy managed to do the same thing under more difficult conditions. He was born at Stoven in Suffolk in 1814, in an old broken-down farmhouse. The land formerly attached to it had been added to a neighbouring farm, and the house fell to the labourers. "My father began a very hard life in very hard times, and I had to endure hardness," he wrote later. He too began to work in early childhood, the common fate of labourer's children at that date, a job known as "keeping crows" or scaring the birds from the newly sown corn. From this humble beginning he proceeded slowly onwards. He became a kitchen boy in a great house, looking after poultry, fetching and carrying, feeding pigs and so on. His next step upwards was to look after yard cattle, and he became a clever feeder. He, too, was fond of reading, and educated himself by reading the farmer's books when he had a job where he had to wait up at night for his employer to return from the pub. By some extraordinary means he taught himself the mysteries of arithmetic.

Finally, he too set up a school, an activity which he combined with several other occupations. He took up bookbinding, learned to stuff birds for sale, and to play the clarinet. He was satisfied with this life, and, just as Dudeney, certain that he had done some good in the world.

To anyone living in the modern world it is almost inexplicable how these men managed to gain the success they did. They cannot have been isolated examples. Unrecorded others, if only a few, must have done the same. In areas where many farms were very small, like Devonshire, it was not absolutely impossible for a labourer, abstemious to the point of self-starvation, to save a tiny sum of money and take a minute holding, from which he might rise to a larger. The majority made no such achievement, but they do not in any age. These were the men celebrated by Oliver Wendell Holmes in the verses:

"Clear the brown path, to meet his coulter's gleam!
Lo! on he comes behind his smoking team
With toil's bright dewdrop on his sunburnt brow,
The lord of earth, the hero of the plough!
These are the hands whose sturdy labour brings
The peasant's food, the golden pomp of kings;
This is the page whose letters shall be seen
Changed by the sun to words of living green."

The half century that passed between the outbreak of the French Wars and the accession of Queen Victoria saw many changes for the men of the land. Many evanescent fortunes were made during the wars and disappeared like snow in summer with the coming of peace. New ideas had to be adopted to meet this disaster, and the resilience of the farmers was demonstrated in their acceptance of the conditions. By 1837 the scene was set for the new era when farming would be prosperous for some decades, but at the same date the labourer was in general suffering from deplorable poverty owing to the inadequacy of his wages, a poverty more severe perhaps than that which physical conditions and ignorance had inflicted upon his ancestors.

CHAPTER SIX

The Victorian Farmer, 1837-1900

THE ACCESSION of Queen Victoria was the beginning of a great age
in English history. Many of Her Majesty's close relations were great
landowners and farmers on the grand scale. She had herself inherited
from her ancestor, George III, the tradition of royal farming, and,
after her marriage to Prince Albert, royal farming spread to many
newly acquired estates and flourished.

Earl Spencer, better known throughout his distinguished career
as Lord Althorp, was a great landowner in Northamptonshire. He was a
cousin of the Queen, and, when he was at Court, the letters he read
first in the morning were those about his pedigree cattle at Wiseton.
In this he was just like Turnip Townshend a hundred years before.

When the Queen came to the throne Lord Althorp was President of
the Smithfield Club. It held an annual dinner each December. At
the function in December 1837 it was Lord Althorp's duty to propose
"Success to the Smithfield Club". He seized the opportunity to point
out that there was room for an association of English farmers that would
devote itself to the general interests of farming. Great progress had
already been made on some farms, but on most, English farming was
still in its infancy. The ordinary English farmer did not know how to
apply science to his practice. Althorp thought that if the results of
experiments were made intelligible to the ordinary man, and the practical nature explained, an improvement would soon take place that few

135

had any conception of. To do this would be the work of the society he had in mind, a society from which politics ought to be rigidly excluded.

The idea was strongly supported by the Duke of Richmond, another royal cousin, by Henry Handley, M.P. for Lincolnshire, and by an imposing list of other great landowners. After a good deal of enthusiastic effort, and, despite some dissentients, the English Agricultural Society was formed. The Queen herself became its patron in 1839, and the name of the embryo society was changed to the Royal Agricultural Society of England. It held its first show at Oxford in that year. Livestock were brought from all over the country for exhibition and a vast quantity of new farming machinery was shown. Ever since then the society has played an immense part in the development of English farming, and has never failed to hold its annual show.

The Royal Society was formed just at the right moment. Nearly forty years of prosperity for the men of the land, with an only occasional season of hard times, were to follow. This period of prosperity opened up wide opportunities for improved farming. The example and precept of the members of this, and the other farming societies, great and small, led the lesser men along the best paths. British livestock were exported to all parts of the world to found the flocks and herds of the empty spaces in America, Africa, Australia and New Zealand. The English arable farmer continued to be the admiration of all comers. Unluckily the uncontrollable element of the weather put a period to this prosperity by continuous rain in the late 1870s, and droughts in the 1890s. To make things worse economic factors, the improvement of transport, the invention of refrigeration, and the flood of food that was imported from America and the Antipodes made heavy contributions to the weight of competition against the home farmer in the last decades of the reign.

Meanwhile the men of the land flourished, and followed gingerly in the footsteps of the great farmers. Only a few of these, selected quite haphazardly from their large number, can be mentioned here. Their work has already been fully discussed in a well-known and widely circulated book.

Royal leadership was not lacking.

The Prince Consort was as enthusiastic a farmer as George III, and his further improvements in the Great Park were a fine example and lead for the high farmers of that time.

The Prince joined the Smithfield Club in 1840, and became an honorary member of the Highland Agricultural Society. He showed two West Highland oxen and a pen of three Suffolk and Bedfordshire pigs at the club show in the year he joined. They were highly commended. This success encouraged him to show every year during the next three decades. The exhibits included Hereford, Devon, Shorthorn and Highland cattle and various classes of pigs.

In addition to exhibiting at the Smithfield Show the Prince showed at the Midland Counties Association at Birmingham, at the Royal Agricultural Society, the Royal Dublin Society, and the Paris International Show of 1855.

Though he was intensely interested in the practice of farming, it is perhaps for the extension and improvement of the existing farms at Windsor that the Prince is best remembered. A dairy homestead was built at Shaw Farm in 1852–54, and a new homestead at the Flemish Farm some years later. Here a herd of pedigree Shorthorns was started. Two Fawsley cows were bought, and Booth's bull "Prince Alfred" was hired. Descendants of these animals have won many awards in the show yards of the great agricultural societies.

The Great Exhibition of 1851 had a livestock department, and the Prince Consort showed a two-year-old Shorthorn bull and two Suffolk boars.

He was not content with confined activities like those of his distinguished ancestor. He must build; so Osborne House was built to his design during the years 1845–49. He built a new homestead on Barton Farm, and another at Alerstone, and he occupied the whole estate with the exception of the latter.

Here a great deal of reclamation work was necessary as it had been nearly a century before in Windsor Great Park. The Prince Consort built roads, drained and planted trees. More than 1,400 miles of covered drains were made besides many miles of ditches.

Besides the Royal Palaces and farmhouses, new cottages, a school and a church were built. A populous and smiling district was created out of a desert. Not content with all this the royal family paid its first visit to Balmoral in 1848, buying it four years later, some 10,000 acres of which 200 acres were under crop. Birkhall, bought for the Prince of Wales, added 6,000 acres of which 400 were arable. The Prince Consort immediately took it in hand. Fences were built to keep the red deer out of the tenants' crops. Farmhouses and cottages were built, and, of course, the Prince was not satisfied until he had taken over a farm here, too. It was Invergelder, between sixty and seventy acres, in six fields, and about ten acres of rough pasture. He found it in a wretched state as left by an impoverished and discouraged tenant.

He grew a green crop on every field, fallow cleaned it, limed it and laid it down to permanent grass, a procedure that could hardly be quarrelled with today. This grassland was stocked with Highland sheep in the summer, and supplied the household with mutton during the visit of the Court in autumn.

To all these must be added the Bagshot and Rapley farms. The Prince Consort expanded the work of "Farmer George" at Windsor and its neighbourhood. He improved the buildings and won prizes with his livestock. He made Osborne and he improved Balmoral. His accomplishment was certainly more diverse and covered a wider area in very different climatic and physical conditions than that of his better-known ancestor. By so much was it the more influential in demonstrating the various ways of improvement that were valuable in different conditions. It was justly said that an account of the work done on the royal farms during the twenty years of the Prince Consort's control would be a history of the agricultural improvements of all the soils of England in that period.

The gentry followed the royal example. Henry Handley, M.P., one of the founders and for a long time a strong supporter of the Royal Society, was the son of a solicitor and banker. He farmed on a large scale, and in the most progressive way at Culverthorpe Hall. He had been educated at Eton and his way of living was that of any landed gentleman. He was one example of many of his class during the first fifty years of Queen Victoria's reign, a class that was an example to all other farmers.

Another such a man, also an early supporter of the "Royal", was Charles Hillyard of Thorpelands, Northamptonshire. He was a friend of Earl Spencer for many years and knew Coke of Holkham and many other famous agriculturalists. He visited both these and many others when he made a tour in the year of the Queen's accession. He recorded his views and opinions in a little book written to instruct and guide his son when he should take over and manage the property. It was so much admired that Hillyard felt obliged to publish it for the general use of farmers. It was entitled *Practical farming and grazing, with observations on*

the breeding and feeding of cattle and sheep. It came out in 1837, an expansion
of a smaller version that was privately printed in 1834.

Capt. Turnill of Reasby in Stainton-by-Langworth, Lincolnshire,
was a prominent improver of Lincoln cattle. His methods have not been
recorded, but his cattle came to be known as the Turnills. The farmers
of this county, where such vast areas of waste and heath had already
been reclaimed, were quick to adopt new things. Philip Pusey, writing of
them in 1842, said that their system was to apply chalk to the newly
broken up land at eighty cubic yards an acre. They dressed their turnip
crops with bones at twelve to sixteen bushels an acre. They kept
large numbers of beasts in yards during the winter and fed oilcake to
make large quantities of rich manure. This system was not known
in the south of England, as Pusey, who lived in Berkshire, was well
aware.

These are a few of the hundreds of rich and enterprising farmers
scattered here and there all over the country. They were the men who
bred the livestock. They drained their land. They used the new
chemical manures and were the first in the field with the new machines.
They were responsible for spreading the improvements that gradually,
during the next forty years, became the general practice of all farmers
worthy of the name.

Enterprising men had been trying the effect of using natural
waste products ever since Elizabeth I's reign. Sir Hugh Plat suggested
many substances then. Early in James I's reign Robert Loder of
Harwell, Berks, had tried using malt dust, the scientific birth of the
place where atomic research is being done today. Bone dust from the
knife handles made at Sheffield had been used in that neighbourhood
in the eighteenth century, and the use of crushed bones developed
from that practice.

The chemical fertilizer industry, now of such large dimensions,
was founded when, in 1840, Lawes and Gilbert set up their factory at
Barking for the manufacture of superphosphate. This factory is still
working and producing today.

Trade with South America was developing, and this placed two
other materials at the disposal of the farmer. Chilian nitrate began to
be imported. Guano from the bird-haunted islands off the coast of
Peru was collected and brought home. British farmers learned to use
it as the Incas were known to have done from the time when the first

Europeans visited their country. The first sample was brought to Europe by Humboldt in 1806, and the early volumes of the Royal Agricultural Society contain many articles about its use and effects. These materials all came into fairly wide use after 1840.

The new machines which have been described in the *Farmers' Tools* were the seed drill and the threshing machine, invented a hundred years before, and developed in the interval. Many new types of ploughs were designed, more especially Ransome's improvements. Barn machinery simplified the preparation of feed for livestock. The portable steam engine was introduced to drive it, and later steam power was adapted for ploughing and other field operations. There were many others.

The new manures, machines and drainage appliances were, of course, only used by the most far-seeing farmers, and progressive people in all walks of life are in the minority. Numbered by hundreds the progressive farmers were only a small proportion of the hundreds of thousands of English farmers. Large occupations were few compared with small, as they have always been in our country. The majority were perhaps between 100 acres and 300 acres in size; and there were a great many ranging from a few acres up to one hundred.

Contemporary description and later recollections of early life show that the tenants of the medium sized farms lived in great simplicity at the beginning of Queen Victoria's reign. They dined in their kitchens, drank nothing but ale, and were only just beginning to take to black coats on Sundays. One such, who was clearly remembered as something of a curiosity in his neighbourhood, occupied 300 acres. He kept this farm in excellent condition with little help of science or machinery. During his lifetime he was regal in his behaviour on market days. Having a large balance with his banker he was under no compulsion to haggle about the price of what he bought, and was only critical of quality. The best was good enough for him.

"If you called upon him, he received you in the kitchen, and a jug of home brewed . . . was placed upon the table, with no apology for not offering wine. He never missed church, and could always be relied upon when money was wanted for any charitable or religious purpose. He was never behind hand with his rent nor ever asked for a reduction. His farm was a sufficient occupation for him. He neither shot nor hunted, though he had opportunities for doing both. He had no books. . . . When he died it was found that he had amassed money; and though he lived into the bad times (of the 1870s) he did not seem to have suffered from them."

Men like this were stubborn in their adherence to the old ways. They did not like to see their daughters doing any ornamental work or their sons going hunting. A certain Mr. Woolcombe noticed that his son had vanished from the farm one morning when the hounds had met in the neighbourhood. "My lord's gone a-hunting," he exclaimed to his wife, with suppressed emotion, "and you knowed of it." He refused to be comforted, and went about the house in the deepest of gloom. Only when his daughter, a girl of nineteen, tucked up her sleeves, went down upon her knees and scrubbed the kitchen floor, was harmony restored to the household.

Farmers like this were content with the same simple fare as their labourers, and smoked their pipes in the kitchen with the men when all had supped together. Their scanty leisure was spent discussing the work done during the day and what must be done on the morrow. Hospitality was generous when the occasion arose, but visitors were infrequent. His neighbours like him, tired after a long day in the field and barn, were thankful to spend their evenings at home with a pipe and a glass in the midst of their families.

The cost of living was a mere trifle for these men. One Midland farmer who occupied 200 acres, and kept forty cows, an enterprise considered a good-sized farm, sat down every Sunday with his family, to a large batter pudding made in a puncheon, with a piece of bacon in the middle. This appetizing mess they ate cold for dinner during the rest of the week. He did not need to buy much. Milk, butter, cheese, bacon, eggs, poultry, pork and vegetables were all produced on the farm, and sufficient of this home produce was appropriated to the producer's table. Beer was brewed and bread was baked at home. It has been estimated that the farmer's net income then was equal to his rent, and this may have been as much as £2 an acre.

On the rare occasions when a well-to-do farmer invited his neighbours to visit him great preparations were made. Everything on the farm had to be in apple-pie order, and a gargantuan feast was provided. The garden was cleaned up, a rare occurrence with a busy farmer who thought more of his fields than the flower and vegetable plot. Stables and rickyard were tidied up. The manes and tails of horses trimmed in readiness for the criticisms, jocular and terse, of his friends. There was a great to do inside the house, which wife and maids made speckless for the inspection of the visiting housewives. All sorts of poultry were cooked. Meat and fruit pies in profusion were prepared. Richly flavoured puddings were made. Mince pies, blanc-mange, jellies, custards, cheese cakes, patties, and no end of other dainties were created. Feasting went on from the snack partaken immediately upon arrival in mid-morning, through the heavy midday dinner until the after-supper dancing. The most was made of a joyous time that could only be repeated infrequently.

The aftermath of a feast like this must have been something to reckon with, but the robust health of the participants could deal with it without too much discomfort. Any sufferings were doubtless counted worth while. There was no let down in going home to the ordinary routine.

Farmers of this class were already beginning to give up dining in the kitchen with their men, and very soon the habit was looked upon as a relic of old times. It lingered on in remote places until the 1850s or later. There were still old squires living in the Yorkshire dales at the date of the Great Exhibition in the Crystal Palace in Hyde Park, whose habits were those of the eighteenth century. It was a "life of coarse and jolly plenty, keeping to the old hours, old drinks and old amusements". The age was one of great contrasts. The old squire's neighbours might be quite up to date in their notions. The age was one of rapid and often destructive change!

A Herefordshire vicarage was an example of modernity in 1847. It contained no bathroom, but the occupants took daily baths. Lighting was by oil lamps and candles. Home baking was done with the help of a widow from a neighbouring cottage. Poultry were kept, but not cows.

The substantial tenant farmer tried to emulate this scale of living. At Holt Farm, near Heathridge, probably a fictional name for Knutsford, Cheshire, the farmhouse parlour was a large room with two casemented windows. Its floor was covered with a home-made carpet of needlework and list. The walls were adorned with one or two family portraits. A pot of flowers rested on Matthew Henry's Bible upon an occasional table. A rug was placed in front of the fireplace, and an oven beside the grate. A crook with a kettle hanging from it simmered over the wood fire, and beside it a game of shovel board was set up. For supper an immense meat pie was served.

Although the farmer's family habitually occupied the parlour as a living-room they did not indulge in extravagant expenditure. Habits of economy were too ingrained for that. One contemporary bit of doggerel verse emphasized this characteristic. The farmer poet exhorted the farmer's family not to indulge his corpse with an expensive funeral.

"Don't go spending money putting me underground,
  The whole thing ought to be done for five to fifteen pound.
  The use of these plumes and hearses and things, I never could see,
  And maybe you'll want the cash when you've not got me.

Then if no labourers wish to do much for the dead,
  Put me in the green cart, and the old mare shall draw me to bed;
  And you and another, not more at most than another or two—
  Shall see the earth close on the coffin, beneath the old yew."

Among the tenant farmers of this class there were some who over estimated the power of their smallish capital and the strength of their own capacity. It was always so, and no doubt always will be so. They were heartily condemned, as having no brains or energy to work their farms, no stock, implements or manure, and consequently no crops worthy of the name. Their farms were too large for them, and their lives one long struggle with the taxpayer, the landlord and the weeds, a struggle in which they were bound to be vanquished at last. They were life's foredoomed failures in farming as they would have been in any other employment.

On the other hand the small farmer on the poor land in the wildest parts of England and Wales was often able to squeeze a living from a quite uncompromising situation. He broke up a little rough moorland for a crop or two, as his ancestors had done for generations. He grew a more handsome crop on the best ground in the vale. He had the right to run a few sheep, cattle or horses, on the hill. These men could hold their own, perhaps for ever. They lived after the ancient fashion, kept a few horses, a cow or two, and a few sheep. They grew a trifle more corn than they could consume at home, and sold small produce, eggs, poultry, cream cheese, sucking pigs, honey and so on.

It was a hard life, but perhaps contented, and therefore happy. Farms of from five acres to one hundred acres were then, as now, to be found almost everywhere. Indeed Eldred F. Walker said that the average size of a holding in England was about sixty acres so recently as 1900. On the smaller of these farms life was very little different from that of the labourers and very different from that of the rich farmer, either tenant or occupying owner.

The Dartmoor peasant lived in a rude cottage, frequently shared with the cattle. It had thick walls of rough granite blocks, a thatch roof. It was a sufficient protection from the weather, but that was as much as could be said for it. A peat fire provided the necessary warmth. The furniture was primitive and scanty. Domestic comforts were unknown. A small patch of rough land, broken up from the adjacent moor, was planted with potatoes and supplied, with the pig, the main elements of the family diet. At harvest the farmer feasted in the field; Christmas festivities were held in the house. These were the only two breaks in the arduous labour of all other times. The life bred a hardy race famed for its strength in spite of eating nothing better, to modern ideas, than barley bread and potatoes with broth and bacon and such vegetables as leeks and onions. This diet changed a little by the end of the nineteenth century. Barley bread had vanished from the table of farmer and worker alike by then, and a little meat was eaten as well as bacon.

Far away from Devonshire a woman farmer owned a farmhouse and some thirty or forty acres of land in Westmorland. The holding carried a hereditary right to a sheep walk above Blue Tarn. It was a grey stone house and a square of farm buildings. Meals were served on polished pewter plates, kept on a dresser when not in use. Meal was kept in a waxed oak awmry, or chest. The lady was keen on a bargain when selling cattle or farm produce, and was competent at all farm work. She led the haymakers with her swift steady rake and noiseless evenness of motion. She was amongst the earliest at market, examining samples of oats, pricing them and turning with grim satisfaction to her own cleaner corn. Though a woman her way of life was that of hundreds of farmers on similar holdings in that county.

It was not difficult to find farms in the Peak of Derbyshire where

"an old oak table, with legs as thick and black as those of an elephant, was spread in the homely house-place (kitchen living-room) for the farmer and his family, wife, children, servants, male and female; and heaped with the rude plenty of beans and bacon, beef and cabbage, fried potatoes and bacon, huge puddings, a table where bread and cheese and beer, and good milk porridge and oatmeal porridge was eaten".

It is evident from these descriptions that this must have been the usual way of life of the farmers on many of the smaller farms that flourished throughout the north, the west, the west Midlands, and elsewhere when Queen Victoria's reign began.

On these farms the master, clad in clouted shoes, fustian coat, blue or black worsted stockings and corduroy breeches, roused the household at five o'clock in the morning. His wife bustled the servant girls at the same time. They had to light fires, sweep the hearth and go to milking, churning and making cheese, just as they had done for hundreds of years. In winter the men and boys had to feed the horses and cows, and prepare for ploughing and leading out manure, to supply the young cattle in the yard with fodder, to chop turnips, mangel-wurzel, carrots, cut hay, boil potatoes for feeding pigs or bullocks, thrash, winnow or sack corn. In summer they worked still longer hours at haymaking and harvest.

These farmers worked with their men and were just as skilful. They worked equally hard. They could plough, drill, harrow, and they spread manure or loaded hay or corn. Often their ancestors had reclaimed the land from the wild by generations of effort.

John Price Sheldon knew one farm in 1893 that had been taken in long before:

> "Two centuries are covered by the tenancy of that farm by the same family; the farm, with the exception of a few enclosures round the homestead was an open more or less rocky and heather clad moor. The successive tenants got out the rocks that impeded the plough and built with them many miles of walls which eventually enclosed the whole farm and parcelled it out into fields. Very nearly the whole of the land was cultivated time upon time . . . very extensively boned and laid down into useful grass land."

By some such slow patient work has much of our land been made.

The family did most of the work on small farms. Children grew up in the tradition of labour, and their delight in helping grown ups to do their work was never discouraged. It was used and praised and was often the child's only possible education for living on holdings far from the village school. Learning was confined to a trifle of the three Rs, if attendance was in any way possible, or, if not, the child was taught some trifling rudiments at home—perhaps. The children grew with a practical understanding of the tasks that daily would confront them throughout their lives, based upon acquaintance with them from childhood:

> "His children were taught honest labour to prize
> Tis industry that health and plenty supplies.
> One son to the plough, soon as able, was sent
> Or in useful field labour his daytime was spent.
>
> The next boy was set the home duties to do
> All the work of the farmyard 'twas his to pursue.
> His work was most useful and varied indeed,
> He'd the cows to look after and the pigs had to feed.
>
> His corn to protect the good farmer took care,
> A scarecrow or two he'd put up here and there;
> When the crops were quite ripe, all assisted to reap,
> And then put it in ricks for the market to keep.
>
> A daughter the good farmer had whose delight
> Was the poultry to feed every morning and night;
> The geese she for Michaelmas fattened to sell
> And the turkeys at Christmas all looked plump and well."

The division of labour on a family farm of the mid-nineteenth century described in these verses was very ancient. Indeed the duties of the various farm servants laid down by John Donaldson in 1866 were very little different from those set out in a thirteenth-century treatise, *Seneschaucie*. The routine was the same though there had been changes. Horses had very generally taken the place of oxen at the plough and for haulage, and steam ploughing and cultivating were coming in.

As the nineteenth century advanced the old habits gradually

changed, though there were still many isolated farms, especially the smaller ones, where habit made an obstacle to any material alteration. Farmers began to dislike the crudity of the environs of their houses. A muddy cattle yard and group of old ramshackle buildings containing discarded implements and other rubbish did not appeal. The better off wanted their windows to look out upon a different view, though there are still farmhouses that have the same higgledy piggledy mess about them.

A poet of the people proclaimed unmusically,

"I hate the murky pool at the back of the stable yard
 For dear though it is to the ducks and geese it has an unpleasant smell."

A Norfolk clergyman put out his doggerel praise of a different scene:

"And this new house, which is but lately built,
 With its smooth lawn extending in the front
 Of some three or four acres, while behind
 Stretch two or three hundred of more fertile ones;
 The dwelling forms of a substantial yeoman,—
 Honest, substantial, hospitable and free. . . .

 Scanning with careful eye his fertile lands,
 Watching the produce of his well-tilled fields,
 And counting every wain that passes by
 Reckoning the profits that his acres yield. . . ."

Careful and ambitious farmers were to be found all over the country, and their efforts were making them prosper. A Devon account for the twenty-five years 1853–77 records the increased yields that were obtained there. A previous tenant only got 10 bushels of wheat an acre in 1852. The next one raised that crop to 40 bushels an acre in 1868 on six acres, and succeeded in growing an average of 22 bushels an acre for the whole twenty-five years upon an annual average of thirty-nine acres. The crop was reaped and tied by hand. The grain was threshed out by a horse wheel that drove a thresher in the barn, but if the straw was wanted for thatching the work was done by hand with flails. The wheat was planted after clover ley, bare fallow, beans or peas, vetches, trifolium, potatoes and roots. Lime and a dung compost was freely used. Some crops were eaten off by sheep in the fold, an ancient method that provided renewed fertility.

The importance of sheep on most farms then and until 1914 has been deplored by A. G. Street in his book *Farmer's Glory*, but it was of real importance in providing manure. It was in 1862 that Professor James Buckman threw up his Chair of Botany and Geology to become a farmer. He rented a farm of 450 acres at Bradford Abbas, between Yetminster and Sherborne in north Dorset. On this farm, as on so many there, the most important crop was sheep, a flock of 500 Dorset Horns and Hampshire Downs being kept. Hereford and Black Scotch cattle (Galloways?) were kept for fattening. A couple of Jersey cows provided milk for the household, as well as butter and a little surplus for the market. A herd of pigs flourished. Half a dozen Shire horses did the ploughing and hauling. There were carriage and riding horses, and sometimes a pupil maintained a hunter. The result was that there was no lack of manure to keep the land in good heart, and Professor Buckman was not only a successful farmer but a frequent contributor to the *Journal of the Bath and West Society*.

Enough cider to last through haysel and harvest was made from a couple of acres of orchard. On this farm until 1873 all the corn was cut by hand except the barley for which a hay mower was used. Twelve men were permanently employed on the farm. Years later the professor's son could remember seeing twenty men reaping corn, and as many women binding behind them. Nostalgically he, when nearly eighty years old, looked back upon this as a romantic and picturesque sight, but consider the cost even in those days of low wages.

Tiny villages like Bradford Abbas were still largely self-sufficient in 1872 as they had been since the beginning of time. Readers of Thomas Hardy will recall his descriptions of life in Wessex. A record of an unidentified Dorset village of that date was preserved by a farmer who thought himself a bit of a historian. One of his brothers ran a farm of which 200 acres were arable, cultivated on the south-western variant of the four-course system. A flying flock of between two and three hundred lambs was bought to eat the turnips and sold when they had done so. A dairy of about forty cows was let to a dairyman in accordance with local custom, and brought in £12 a cow, a certain income of £480 a year. All this livestock provided plenty of manure.

The farm was one of four grouped round a village of 600 inhabitants. The local bigwigs were the landlord, parson and schoolmaster. The four farmers came next with their carters, shepherds and labourers. The miller ground the farmers' corn into flour. Two bakers made bread and cakes for those who did not do their own baking. A butcher killed the local bullocks, and there was a pig killer and pork butcher.

The wheelwright made the wagons. Two blacksmiths shod the horses and one of these farriers acted as veterinary surgeon. A local man thatched the stacks and the buildings when they needed it. Another made the wattle hurdles for the sheep fold. Baskets for all purposes, including cradles, were made by another villager. There was a mason and two carpenters who sawed their own timber over a saw pit, and made coffins as required in addition to their ordinary work. In spare moments they made furniture for local use.

The general shop provided groceries and any other imported needs. There was a village tailor and a village dressmaker. The weighty products of the village shoemaker were as stiff as leather could be, heavy with innumerable nails, and guaranteed to keep out the wet for ever if a man was strong enough in the leg to lift them. The carrier fetched anything that was wanted from the nearest town, and his cart was a passenger vehicle for anyone who wished to travel abroad.

Cattle disease broke out in the early 1870s, and was the beginning of a series of disasters that befell farmers during that decade. They culminated in the continuous rain of 1879, when the corn rotted on the ground, sheep died by the thousand, and everything seemed to combine to beat the rural community to its knees. One thing did not happen. Though a dead specimen of a Colorado beetle was seen by the Rev. B. J. Armstrong at Norwich in 1877, and the Government had warned the farmers to look out for them, this affliction was not added to the others.

One thing was emphasized by nearly all those who gave evidence to the Richmond Commission. The perennial complaint that the men were not so skilful and industrious as their forefathers, was a constant grievance with most of the farmers and land agents who were questioned. Doubtless this was as true as it had been since the days of Cincinnatus. It has continued until the present day, and will probably be repeated in the generations to come. A. G. Street's novel *The Gentleman of the Party* has amply demonstrated its fallacy.

Richard Jefferies's character, John Brown, was one of these men. His slouching walk, with knees bent, diminished his height and appearance; he really was the full size. Every inch of his frame had been slowly welded together by ceaseless work, continual life in the open air and coarse hard food. "This is what makes a man hardy. This is what makes a man able to stand almost anything, and gives a power of endurance that can never be obtained by any amount of gymnastic training."

Amongst the village people old fashions lingered on into the 1880s as Thomas Hardy's Wessex novels show. In Winscombe, a village on the Mendip Hills, both old and young were then seen daily who might have been the originals of those rustic figures immortalized several decades before by Bewick and Pyne. The ploughman, the hedger, the woodman, the shepherd, the sower, the reaper with tied belt and light clothing, the old man breaking stones by the roadside, the old woman in her scarlet cloak, farm labourers, milkmaids, haymakers, village children, rustic horses and rusty harness, old-fashioned cows, pigs and poultry were all still as primitive and picturesque as the great nineteenth-century painters of English landscape and rural life could have wished or imagined. In villages like this the farming was still rather backward. Elsewhere, even close by, the standards were high. The excellent farming of the few leaders who had shown the way at the beginning of Queen Victoria's reign had spread throughout the country during the first forty years of her sovereignty, and fine farms were to be found everywhere, but in villages like Winscombe the plough only turned over a few inches of the surface year after year and below this was a hard pan that had not been disturbed, only more firmly compressed with each year from time immemorial. The meadows were as little drained as the arable and it was said that the industrious mole did more than the farmer to top dress the land. The farmers exercised little foresight. In times of plenty there was waste; in times of scarcity there was want.

Many of the better-off farmers have been condemned for their unwillingness or inability to adopt the best methods of their day. They were picturesque enough to the eyes of an inexperienced townsman. They dressed in a hard hat and gaiters, rode to hounds once or twice a week, a proceeding that had been severely criticized by their elders a generation before. They were content to plod along in the traditional way, accepting reluctantly and with pessimism the new tools, new manures and feeding stuffs that the new age was putting at their disposal. Nature failed them and the rather easy good times vanished. There was little to bring to market. The unspeakable weather had ruined the crops. Epidemic disease reduced the livestock. Prices were falling in face of the new competition of food imported from overseas. The farmer did not know where to turn. He was a rugged individualist who had no taste for co-operation in order to cheapen his buying and to maintain his markets. He had trusted that the good times would go on for ever, and had lived up to his income, but twenty years of hardship were to teach him an unforgettable lesson.

There is, however, one great advantage in farming. If you cannot sell the produce at a good price you can at least live on some of it. Many did so, and, in addition, managed to make their work a business. They were the average farmers who continued to live as simply and to work as hard as their ancestors.

The day began at five o'clock in the morning as it always had. At breakfast fat bacon and bread was eaten with an appetite resulting from two or three hours in the crisp morning air. The farmer drank a pint or so of strong beer with it. He followed this with bread and butter and tea. After breakfast he set out to look after the men, or to work beside them. At midday he came home to the old-established dinner of bacon and greens, though fairly well-to-do farmers had a joint of beef or mutton two or three times a week, with plenty of vegetables from their gardens. Supper was at six, or any convenient time at busy seasons.

This was the daily life of a middle-class farmer. He dressed in no more luxurious style than he lived, but he would have good quality in his clothes. Farmers did not wear a shirt front, that abominable Victorian garment, no studs, rings or hide gloves. These were gentlemen's fashions. The farmer wore heavy thick substantial boots. He had to because it has been said a good farmer never walked less than ten miles a day over his fields. The average ploughman walked no less than sixteen doing a day's work. This type of farmer was "not half so smartly dressed as a well-paid mechanic, and far behind the draper's assistant in style" at the date of Queen Victoria's Jubilee in 1887.

A favourite improvement in the farmer's home was to close in the great open fireplace of the kitchen living-room, and put in a coal-burning grate. One who had done this had a pair of brass candlesticks and other brass ornaments on the mantel with some china figures.

Above it was a narrow looking-glass. An old "grandfather" clock stood in the corner. In the middle of the room was a solid oak table, and at either side of the fire was a stiff-backed wooden chair. The window seat was a pleasant place in summer. A massive dresser and a corner cupboard filled up the rest of the room. A good many rooms like it can still be found in old farmhouses. There was a parlour in his house, and two fair-sized bedrooms, furnished with wooden four-poster beds. Above these were the attic rooms for the maids. At one end of the house was a one-storey building containing a cheese loft, a dairy, the kitchen, cellar and woodshed.

Fine farming and devotion to their estates was still to be found among landowners all over the country in spite of the depression. Edward, Prince of Wales, set a fine example. Arnold Bennett was enthusiastic about the care and maintenance at Sneyd in 1902. "Every hedge and ditch and gate and stile was in that ideal condition of correctness which denotes that a great landowner is exhibiting the beauties of scientific farming for the behoof of the villagers." George Meredith's *Egoist* was such another, and their names and descriptions are scattered through the pages of Rider Haggard's *Rural England*, 1902, and Sir Daniel Hall's *Pilgrimage of British Farming 1910–1912*, 1913, just as they had been in James Caird's *English Agriculture in 1850–51*, 1852, or in Arthur Young's *Tours* in the eighteenth century.

Always there are some who are over enthusiastic and misguided. They are typified in another profession in Bernard Shaw's *Doctor's Dilemma*. An amateur farmer, overly scientific, aroused Richard Jefferies's scorn. Cecil, a man of capital, had gone into farming as a commercial speculation hoping to make cent per cent. He began in the midst of the fervour of novelty. He grubbed up all the hedges and threw all his arable into one vast field. He drained it six feet deep at enormous cost. He built one engine shed with a centrifugal pump, which forced water from the stream . . . over the entire property and supplied the house. He laid a tramway across the estate and sent the men to work in trucks. The chaff cutters, root pulpers, winnowing machine—everything was driven by steam. A fine set of steam-ploughing tackle was constantly at work often bringing the sterile subsoil to the surface. Barges full of manure and carts full of coal were forever arriving. Machines of every class and character were provided. New buildings for the livestock and new cottages for the men (this is the proper order of precedence) were put up. And last, and apparently worst, a complete system of book-keeping was organized. All went well until the slump and then this unfortunate realized that his improvements had been too hastily made. Instead of gradually introducing the new he had sunk all his capital at once, and had nothing left with which to meet the new day. However, he was optimistic enough to believe that good times would return in the ordinary cycle of events. Nothing could convince him that English agriculturists ought to go on using wooden ploughs, wearing smock frocks, and plodding round and round in the same old track for ever. A great contrast to this man was one, Hodson, an agricultural genius of the old style, who made his fortune by the most stringent economy, combined with a daring speculation in taking a large farm when prices were high. Managed in the same slow and gradual way of development as the smaller one, this was able to withstand the disasters when they overwhelmed others.

Innumerable books of memoirs, of nostalgic reminiscence, dealing with farmers and farm life half a century ago have been published in the past twenty years. Almost as many were published contemporarily between 1890 and 1910, as well as a myriad of pamphlets, books and so on, dealing with the plight of farmers and their occupation then. They are far too numerous for quotation, but a few of the writers are, H. G. Massingham, the high priest of the old ways; C. Henry Warren; Flora Thompson, whose book *Lark Rise to Candleford* became a modest best seller. Any selection is bound to omit somebody's favourite book and our excuse must be the wide choice there is.

Times were bad and complaint was general, but some of the memoir writers recall details of generous meals served in their parents' and grandparents' farmhouses. All of us who had farming ancestry of that date have similar memories.

Mathena Bloomfield described a farmhouse tea-table.

"It was a pleasant sight; snowy white cloth, gleaming silver, pink and white tea service, and the food looked so good. There was stiff shiny pork cheese, a plate of pink and white ham, cut very thinly and decorated with parsley; a glass dish of pickled white herrings, also adorned with parsley; a damson cheese, flanked by a jug of thick cream; a dish of rich brown gingerbread, two plates of home baked bread and butter, stewed pears and custard—a lovely tea."

This does not sound much like poverty or semi-starvation, but most of the food could have been produce of the farm. A meal like this would seem to have made supper unnecessary, but as a rule they had a cold supper of meat and pickles, celery and cheese, cake and jam tarts. As a special addition there might be a fruit tart with cream. A specimen dinner was roast leg of mutton, mashed turnips, brussel sprouts, baked potatoes and caper sauce, followed by a hot raspberry jam rolly-poly and cream. Whatever their worries these people did not starve.

Towards the end of the nineteenth century the ranks of farmers included many men of substance like these. Others were gentlemen farmers like Arthur H. Savory's family of Badsey in Worcestershire, who did a great deal for that part of the country by organizing the Badsey Growers, and in other ways. There was also the famous Bomford family in that county, where they had been farming for nearly a century. These are only two of the numerous company who were leading the way in the rehabilitation of English farming after the climatic disasters from which they had suffered.

Others in a descending scale farmed lesser acreages and lived in a more modest style, until at the lowest level the farmer was able to live in a very little, if any, better state than the worker. For them the clean scrubbed table in the kitchen was the dining table, and though father might sit in a wooden armchair, the children were ranged on benches at either side.

Savory had a great deal to say for the labourers of Worcestershire. Those born in the Vale of Evesham were mostly tall and powerful men, and all could read and write, even those who had grown up before the days of compulsory education. They were highly skilled in all the most difficult agricultural operations, and it was easy to find amongst them good thatchers, drainers, hedgers, ploughmen and stockmen. From his staff Savory selected one to be bailiff. He was William Bell, a blue-eyed, dark-haired, tall, lean and muscular man, the picture of energy and the prime of life. Straightforward, unselfish, a natural leader of men, courageous and untiring, he became devoted to his employer and remained his right hand, dear friend and practical advisor in the practical working of the farm throughout the twenty years that followed.

Possibly the Worcestershire labourers were exceptionally big men.

In other respects they were no different from the labourers elsewhere throughout the country. They were skilled, willing and industrious, though wages were low and hours were long. They do not seem to have been discontented with their lot in life. A little more money would have been welcome, and then they would have been satisfied. Masters and men were well known to each other. They had probably been brought up together, and despite their rather feudal recognition of their respective stations in life, few problems in connexion with them ever entered their heads. They accepted conditions that were as natural as the nature around them, or so some would have us believe.

The day's work was much the same as it had always been. The farm-house woke at six in the morning and some of the teamsmen had been at work since half past four. The horses had been watered and fed, cleaned and harnessed, and were out at work by six o'clock. The cows had been milked and fed by that time, and the house was readied for the family. The day-long work went on till dark and later.

Some of the more arduous tasks were relieved by the company in which they were done. Haymaking and harvest were two of these. The work was hard and the hours were long especially if the new mowing and reaping machines were not used, and there were such farms at the end of the century. Men and women laboured together. Elder children worked with them and younger children cared for the babies in a corner cf the field, under the shade of a hedgerow tree where the cask of ale or cider was set for all to drink from. It was a merry time, though doubtless some of the merriment was stimulated by strong ale. "There was singing that might pass for screaming, and laughter that burst forth in peals and shouts; and talking in every variety of key from the rough commanding halloo of the farmer, issuing his commands from one end of the field to the other," and the shrill cries of the children of all ages.

In some places the village flower show or annual feast was followed by a dance, which was considered an appropriate ending for a some-what hectic day. It put everyone in a good temper and cleared up all the disappointments and ill feeling consequent upon failure to win a prize or for some other reason. What dances were danced on the greens-ward will never be known, but Edward G. Thompson thought they were not dances at all. "A man just chose a woman and romped with her. The chief pleasure of it was that he could hug a woman who would only allow that sort of thing at a dance. Anyhow the women enjoyed it," or so he believed.

Rambunctious frivolities of this kind, allowable once a year, were not popular with the more sedate, and were a good deal toned down in a great many places. The old-time harvest home, that some are trying to revive today, had sadly degenerated. It had become a harvest festival of tea and cake at sixpence a head, consumed in the schoolroom, with a choral service and a sermon in the church. Village weddings, too, had become sedate and quiet. There was little feasting and no dancing. There were no more shearing feasts. The old village revels, wrote Baring Gould despondently, linger on in the most emaciated and expiring semblence of the old feast.

And so we come to the end of Queen Victoria's reign. Farmers were by then beginning to overcome the effects of the depressive years. There had been much laying down of land to pasture and changing over from grain to milk production. In this and other ways the men of the land had shown once again their resilience in face of difficulties arising out of changes in economic conditions which were outside their control, but to which they were able to adapt themselves.

Two great surveys of farming were made then and soon after. Rider Haggard made the one; Sir Daniel Hall the other ten years later. Both show that there were successful men as always, who were a pattern to their neighbours, and whose achievements were as worthy of record as any that had gone before. There was also the great body of ordinary farmers whose holdings were on the small side. They occupied farms of a few acres up to one hundred or even two hundred acres. They lived simply and worked hard. They knew that they were working under severe handicaps but they carried on, keeping the foundations of their craft sound enough to face the crisis that was to come when they would once again be called upon to do all that was possible in our small island to supply its vast population with a larger proportion of its food. The excellence of their work was to be demonstrated in the trials of war.

The farmer's men carried on as the farmer did. His lot was hard and his reward was minute, but love of the work was ingrained in both and one could not have kept going without the other. England has always had reason to be proud of her men of the land.

APPENDIX

Authorities for Chapter One

ASHLEY, W. J., The Bread of our Forefathers, 1928.

BLOMEFIELD, J. C., History of the present Deanery of Bicester, Oxon, 1882. Pt. VI.

BLOMEFIELD, J. C., A History of Finmere (Oxfordshire), 1877.*

BRADLEY, HARRIET, The Enclosures in England and Economic Reconstruction, Columbia Studies in History, Economics and Public Law, LXXX, 1918.

BRAYSHAW, THOMAS AND ROBINSON, RALPH M., History of the Ancient Parish of Giggleswick, Yorks, 1932.

BRODERICK, G. C., English Land and English Landlords, 1881.

BRYNE, M. ST. CLARE, Elizabethan life in Town and Country, 1925.

CAMPBELL, MILDRED, The English Yeoman under Elizabeth and the Early Stuarts, 1942.

CRUMP, W. B., The Ancient Highways of the Parish of Halifax, 1929.

DRUMMOND, J. C. AND WILBRAHAM, ANNE, The Englishman's Food, 1939.

[ERNLE, LORD] PROTHERO, R. E., Agriculture and Gardening in Shakespeare's England; an account of the life and manners of his age, ed. by Sir Sidney Lee, 1917.

[ERNLE, LORD] PROTHERO, R. E., The Enclosure of Open Field Farms, Jour. Min. Agric., Dec. 1920 and Jan. 1921.

[ERNLE, LORD] PROTHERO, R. E., The Land and its People, n.d., c. 1925.

[ERNLE, LORD] PROTHERO, R. E., English Farming, Past and Present, 1932.

FARRER, WILLIAM, The Court Rolls of the Honour of Clithero in the County of Lancaster, 1897.

FITZHERBERT, Husbandry, 1523, in Certain Ancient Tracts concerning the management of landed property reprinted, 1767.

GOULD, S. BARING, Old Country Life, 1895.

GRAINGER, FRANCIS, Agriculture in Cumberland in Ancient Times. Trans. Cumbl'd and Westl'd Antiq. Soc. N.S. 1,* 1909.

HALL, HUBERT, Society in the Elizabethan Age, 1901.

HARRISON, WILLIAM, Harrison's Description of England in Shakespeare's Time, ed. by F. J. Furnivall, 1877–81.

JUDGES, A. V., The Elizabethan Underworld, 1930.

KENNEDY, W. P., Parish Life under Queen Elizabeth, 1914.

LENNARD, REGINALD, The alleged exhaustion of the soil in Medieval England, Economic Jour., March 1922.

LISTER, JOHN, West Riding Session Rolls, 1597/8–1602. Yorkshire Arch. and Top. Assn. Record Series III, 1888. N.B. Many other Session Rolls have been printed that indicate a similar incidence of petty crime all over the country.

MARCHAM, W. McB. AND F., Court Rolls of the Bishop of London's Manor of Hornsey, 1603–1701, 1929.

ORLEBAR, FREDERICKA ST. JOHN, The Orlebar Chronicles in Bedfordshire and Northamptonshire, 1930.

ROWSE, A. H., The England of Elizabeth, 1950.

SHARP, MARY, A Record of the Parish of Padworth (Berks) and its Inhabitants, 1911.

SHEPPARD, H. BAYARD, Courts Leet and the Court Leet of the Borough of Taunton. Somerset Arch. and Nat. Hist. Soc., 1909.

* These and the other local histories quoted are a sample of the innumerable works of the sort that contain detailed reprints of contemporary documents or parts of them. Local antiquarian and archaeological societies' annual transactions are another fruitful source for these documents, amongst which there is a marked degree of similarity.

SIMKHOVITCH, V. J., Hay and History. Political Science Quarterly, Sept. 1913.

SMITH, R. TROW, English Husbandry, 1951.

SURFLET, RICHARD, Maison Rustique or the Country Ferme, 1600.

THORNBURY, G. W., Shakespeare's England, or Sketches of our social Life in the reign of Queen Elizabeth, 1856.

TROTTER, ELEANOR, Seventeenth century life in a country parish, 1919. Though this is specifically seventeenth century it applies equally to the sixteenth century, cf. Ware below.

TUPLING, G. H., The Economic History of Rossendale, 1927.

TUSSER, THOMAS, Five Hundred Points of Good Husbandry, 1577, ed. by William Mavor, 1812.

WARE, SEDLEY LYNCH, The Elizabethan Parish in its Ecclesiastical and Financial Aspects (Baltimore), 1908.

WHITNEY, MILTON, The Yield of Wheat in England during seven centuries. Science, LVIII, 26th Oct., 1923.

WOODWARD, MARCUS, The Countryman's Jewel, 1934.

Authorities for Chapter Two

ASHLEY, W. J., The Bread of our Forefathers, 1928.

BERRY, M., A. Comparative View of the Social Life of England and France, 1828. The sketch of Squire Hastings is said to have been drawn by the Earl of Shaftsbury. Berry cited the Connoisseur, III, No. 81.

BLOMEFIELD, J. C., As Chapter I.

BRETON, NICHOLAS, Fantasticks, 1626.

CAMPBELL, MILDRED, The English Yeoman, 1942.

COATE, MARY, Social Life in Stuart England, 1924.

CUNNINGHAM, W., Alien Immigrants to England, 1879.

DAVIES, GODFREY, The Early Stuarts, 1603–1660, 1937.

ELAND, G., Old Works and Past Days in Rural Buckinghamshire, 1923.

FLETCHER, J. S., Memorials of a Yorkshire Parish (Darrington).

FOX, EVELYN, The Diary of an Elizabethan Gentlewomen. Trans. Roy. Hist. Soc., 3rd Set, II, 1908.

FUSSELL, G. E., The English Rural Labourer, 1949.

FUSSELL, G. E., The Farmer's Tools, 1500–1900, 1952, Chap. III.

GARNIER, RUSSELL M., History of the English Landed Interest, Vol. I, 1892.

GODFREY, ELIZABETH, Home Life of the Stuarts, 1603–1649, 1903.

GODFREY, ELIZABETH, Social Life under the Stuarts, 1904.

GOOGE, BARNABY, The Whole Art and Trade of Husbandry, 1614.

HILL, JOHN H., History of the Hundred of Garfree, Leics, 1875.

HOBY, Diary of Lady Margaret, 1599–1605, ed. by Dorothy M. Meads, 1930.

JONSON, BEN, Every Man out of his Humour, 1599. Act I, sc. i.

JOSSELIN, The Diary of the Rev. Ralph, 1616–1683, ed. by E. Hockcliffe. Camden, 3rd Series, XV, 1908.

LODER, ROBERT, Farm Accounts, 1610–1620, ed. by G. E. Fussell. Camden, 3rd Series, LIII, 1936.

MACKIE, J. D., Cavalier and Puritan, 1926.

MARKHAM, GERVASE, The English Husbandman, 1613.

MARKHAM, GERVASE, Farewell to Husbandry, 1638.

MASCALL, LEONARD, The Government of Cattel, 1596.

MAXEY, EDWARD, A New Instruction of Plowing and Setting Corn, 1601.

MUFFITT, THOMAS, Health's Improvement, c. 1600, cited in Parmalee Prentice, Hunger and History, 1939.

NEWMAN, L. F., Some notes on food and dietetics in the sixteenth and seventeenth centuries. Jour. Roy. Anthropological Soc. 76, 1946.

NORDEN, JOHN, Speculi Britanniae Pars, Essex, 1594. Intro. by Sir Henry Ellis, Camden Soc., 1840.

NORDEN, JOHN, Speculi Britanniae Pars altera, or a Delineation of Northamptonshire, 1720. This survey was made in 1590 but was not printed until 130 years later.

NORDEN, JOHN, The Surveyor's Dialogue, 1610.

OVERBURY, SIR THOMAS, Characters, 1614–16.

PEACHAM, HENRY, The Worth of a Penny, c. 1620.

PLAT, SIR HUGH, The New and Admirable Art of Setting Corn, 1600.

PLATTES, GABRIEL, A Discovery of Infinite Treasure, 1639.

ROBERTS, GEORGE, The Social History of the People of the Southern Counties of England, 1856.

ROUS, JOHN, The diary of, 1625–1642, ed. by Mary Anne Everett Green. Camden Soc. LXVI, 1856.

SHAKESPEARE, Love's Labour Lost, Act. V, sc. ii.

Shuttleworth's of Gawthorpe Hall, The House and Farm Accounts of, ed. by John Harland. Chetham Soc. XLI, 1856.

SMITH, R. TROW, English Husbandry, 1951.

STEPHENS, JOHN, Essays and Characters, 1615.

WESTON, SIR RICHARD, Discours of Husbandry, 1645?

WHITAKER, W. B., Sunday in Tudor and Stuart Times, 1933.

WILLAN, T. S., The Parliamentary Surveys for the N.R. of Yorkshire. Yorkshire Arch. Jour., XXXI, 1934.

YARRANTON, ANDREW, The great improvement of lands by clover, 1663.

Authorities for Chapter Three

ASHTON, JOHN, Social Life in the reign of Queen Anne, 1882.

AULT, NORMAN, Seventeenth century lyrics, 1928.

B.F., The Office of the Good Housewife, 1672.

BAXTER, THE REV. RICHARD, Last Treatise, 1691, ed. by F. G. Powicke.

BLENCOWE, R. B., in Sussex Arch. Collecs., 1849, cited in Adelaide Gossett, Shepherds of Britain, 1911.

BLOMEFIELD, J. C., History of Bicester, 1882, Pt. V.

BLOOMFIELD, J. C., History of Finmere, 1887.

BRYANT, ARTHUR, The England of Charles II, 1934.

CAPES, W. W., Scenes of Rural life in Hampshire among the Manors of Bramshott, 1901.

CATHCART, EARL, Jethro Tull, his life, times and teaching. Jour. R.A.S.E., 1891.

CLARK, G. N., The Later Stuarts, 1660–1712, 1934.

CURTLER, W. H. R., Victoria County History of Nottinghamshire, Vol. II, 1910.

DELMEGE, ANTHONY, Towards National Health, 1931.

ERNLE, LORD, The Land and its People, 1925.

FIENNES, CELIA, The Journeys of, ed. by Christopher Morris, 1949.

FUSSELL, G. E. AND ATWATER, V. G. B., Farmer's Goods and Chattels, 1500–1800. History Vol. XX, N.S., Dec. 1935.

FUSSELL, G. E., Pioneer Farming in the late Stuart Age, Jour. R.A.S.E., 1940.

FUSSELL, G. E., After the Restoration; Stuart Squires, Manors and Farms, Agriculture, Sept. 1951.

FUSSELL, G. E., The Farmer's Tools, 1500–1900, 1952, Chap. III.

GREGORY, J. W., The Story of the Road, 1931.

GREEN, J. R., Short History of the English People, ed. of 1907. The entry of Charles II into Whitehall marked a deep and lasting change in the temper of the English people. With it modern England began. The influence which had up to this time moulded our history, the theological influence of the Reformation, the monarchial influence of the new kingship, the feudal influence of the Middle Ages, the yet earlier influence of tradition and custom, suddenly lost its power over the minds of men. From the moment of the Restoration we find ourselves all at once among currents of thought and activity which have gone on widening and deepening from that time to this. The England around us became our own England.

HARPER, CHARLES G., The Bunyan Country, 1928.

HAVERGILL, FRANCIS T., Records of the Parish of Upton Bishop, Herefordshire, 1883.

HEWITT, WILLIAM, The History of Antiquities of the Hundred of Compton, Berks, 1844.

HUMPHREYS, A. L., East Hendred, a Berkshire Parish, 1923.

HEWETSON, ANTHONY, Social Life and National Movements in the seventeenth century. The diary of Thomas Bellingham, an officer under William III, 1908.

KEITH, THEODORA, Commercial relations of England and Scotland, 1603–1707, 1910.

LENNARD, R. V., Rural Northampton under the Commonwealth. Oxford Studies in Social and Legal History, Vol. V, No. 10, 1916.

LENNARD, R. V. English Agriculture under Charles II. Economic History Rev. Vol. IV, 1932.

LISLE, EDWARD, Observations in Husbandry, 1757.

LODGE, ELEANOR C. (ed.), The Account Book of a Kentish Estate, 1616–1704, 1927.

MACAULAY, History of England, 1848, Chap. III.

OGG, DAVID, England in the reign of Charles II, 1934.

The Parish Priest. Quarterly Review, Oct. 1857.

POPE, ALEXANDER, A Discourse on Pastoral Poetry, 1716.

RHYS, J. P., The Countryside of the Seventeenth Century. Jour. Land Agents Society, Dec. 1931.

RYAN, P. F. WILLIAMS, Stuart Life and Manners, 1912.

ROGERS, MR., An Historical Account of Mr. Rogers' Three Years Travels over England and Wales, 1694.

SHARP, MARY, A Record of the Parish of Padworth and its Inhabitants, 1911.

SHELDON, GILBERT, From Trackway to Turnpike, 1928. Chaps. VII and VIII.

SIDNEY, W. C., Social Life in England from the Restoration to the Revolution, 1660–1690, 1892.

STEER, W., Farm and Cottage Inventories of Mid-Essex, 1635–1749, 1950.

TAYLOR, RANDALL, Discourse on the Growth of England, 1689.

TRAILL, Social England, Vol. V, 1896.

TREVELYAN, G. M., The England of Queen Anne, 1934.

TROTTER, ELEANOR, Seventeenth Century Life in a Country Parish, 1919.

UNWIN, GEORGE, Studies in Economic History. The collected papers of, ed. by R. H. Tawney, 1927.

WESTERFIELD, R. B., Middlemen in English Business, 1660–1707, 1910.

WILLEY, BASIL, The Seventeenth Century Background, 1934. Review in *Times Literary Supplement*, 19th April, 1934.

Authorities for Chapter Four

ALSOPP, H., The Change to Modern England, 1922.

ANON., The Present State of England, 1750.

ASHLEY, W. J., The Economic Organization of England, 1916.

ASHLEY, W. J., The Bread of our Forefathers, 1928.

ASHLEY, W. J., The Place of Rye in the History of English Food. Economic Journal, 1921.

ASHTON, John, Old Times, a picture of social life at the end of the eighteenth century, 1885.

AUBREY, JOHN, Old Manners and Customs, 1768.

BAKER, JOHN, Diary of, Sussex Arch. Collec., Vol. 52.

BATCHELOR, THOMAS, General View of the Agriculture of Bedford, 1808.

BERNARD, SIR THOMAS, Pleasure and Pain (1780–1818), ed. by J. Bernard Baker, 1930.

BLYTH, SAM, Inventory of the Household Goods on Mr. Sam Blyth's Farm taken 7th and 8th July, 1796. Colchester Museum.

BUTTER, JOSEPHINE E., Memoirs of John Grey of Dilston, 1869.

BUER, M. C., Health, Wealth and Population in the early days of the Industrial Revolution, 1926.

CLAPHAM, J. H., The growth of an agrarian proletariat. Cambridge Historical Journal, 1923. The increase in proletarians is here assessed as numerically small.

COLE, JOHN, Popular Biography of Northamptonshire, 1839.

CRABBE, GEORGE, The Village, 1783.

CUNNINGHAM, W., The Growth of English Industry and Commerce, Vol. II, 1912.

DAY, THOMAS, Sandford and Merton, 1783.

ELLIS, WILLIAM, The Farmer's Instructor, 1747.

ELLMAN, JOHN, Memoirs of, in Baxter's Library of Agricultural and Horticultural Knowledge, 1834.

ERNLE, LORD, English farming, past and present, 1932.

FIELDING, HENRY, Joseph Andrews, 1742.

FIELDING, HENRY, Tom Jones, 1749.

FUSSELL, G. E. AND ATWATER, V. G. B., Farmer's Goods and Chattels 1500–1800. History. Dec. 1935.

FUSSELL, G. E., English Rural Labourer, 1949.

GARNIER, RUSSELL M., History of the English Landed Interest, Vol. II, 1893.

GEORGE, DOROTHY, England in Transition, 1931.

GREEN, J. H., Short History of the English People, 1907 ed.

GROSE, FRANCIS, The Olio, 1792.

GROSLEY, M., A Tour to London, tr. by Thos. Nugent, 1765.

HAMMOND, J. L. AND BARBARA, The Village Labourer, 1911.

HASBACH, WILLIAM, The English Agricultural Labourer, tr. by Ruth Kenyon, 1908.

HOBZMEN, JAMES W., The Nabobs in England, 1760–85, 1926.

HONE, WILLIAM, Everyday Book, July 1926.

JEKYLL, GERTRUDE, Old West Surrey, 1904.

KALM, PEHR, Account of his visit to England in 1748.

LEVY, HERMAN, Large and Small Holdings, tr. by Ruth Kenyon, 1911.

Liberal Land Committee, The Land and the Nation. Rural Report of the, 1923.

LLOYD, E. WALFORD, John Ellman of Glynde. Jour. R.A.S.E., 1928.

LOWER, RICHARD, Stray Leaves, 1862.

LUCAS, JOHN, History of Warton Parish (1710–1740) ed. by John Rawlinson Ford and J. A. Fuller-Maitland, 1931. Reviewed in *Manchester Guardian*, 11th Jan., 1932. Unfortunately the editors cut out most of the parts about farming.

[MACKAY, JOHN], A Journey through England, 1714.

McQUOID, PERCY, A History of English Furniture, Vol. III, 1906.

MURALT, MONS, Letters describing the English and French Nations, 1726.

PARTRIDGE, CHARLES, A Suffolk Yeoman's Household Goods, 1789. Notes and Queries, Vol. 192.

PARTRIDGE, CHARLES, A Suffolk Yeoman's pre-1790 books. Notes and Queries, Vol. 194.

PLUMB, J. H., Sir Robert Walpole and Norfolk Husbandry. Econ. Hist. Rev. 2nd Ser., Vol. V.

REES, ARTHUR J., Old Sussex and her diarists, 1929.

RITCHES, NAOMI, The Agricultural Revolution in Norfolk, 1937.

RODGERS, BETSY, Cloak of Charity, 1949.

ROGERS, A. G. L., Was rye the ordinary food of the English? Economic Jour., 1922.

SMOLLETT, TOBIAS, Humphrey Clinker, 1771.

STROUD, DOROTHY, Capability Brown, 1950.

UNWIN, GEORGE, Samuel Oldknow and the Arkwrights, 1924.

WATSON, JOHN, Annals of a quiet valley, 1894.

WATSON, J. A. SCOTT, Bakewell's Legacy, Jour. R.A.S.E., 1928.

YOUATT, WILLIAM, Cattle, 1834.

YOUNG, ARTHUR, Six Weeks Tour, 2nd ed., 1769.

YOUNG, ARTHUR, Annals of Agriculture, XVII, 1792.

Authorities for Chapter Five

Agriculture, Board of, Individual surveys of each county by various authors issued under the title of General View of the Agriculture of the County of . . . revised editions between 1797 and 1815.

Agriculture, Board of, Agricultural State of the Kingdom in Jan., Feb. and March, 1816.
ANON., From the Plough Tail to the College Steps being the first twenty-nine years in the life of a Suffolk Farmer's Boy, 1885.
CAMERON, H. C., Sir Joseph Banks, the Autocrat of Philosophers, 1744–1820, 1952, Chap. VI.
CLARKE, SIR E., Agriculture and the House of Russell, Jour. R.A.S.E., 1891.
"The Druid" (H. H. Dixon), Saddle and Sirloin, ed. of 1895.
ELIOT, GEORGE, Adam Bede, 1859.
ERNLE, LORD, English Farming Past and Present, 1932.
FUSSELL, G. E., The English Rural Labourer, 1949.
GARNIER, RUSSELL M., History of the English Landed Interest, 1892, Chap. XV.
GOEDE, C. A. G., The Stranger in England, 1812, 1813.
HAMMOND, J. L. AND BARBARA, The Village Labourer, 1911.
LOUDON, J. C., Encyclopaedia of Agriculture, 2nd ed., 1831.
MARSHALL, WILLIAM, The Rural Economy of the West of England including Devonshire, Vol. I, 1796.
CHARLES KNIGHT, Penny Magazine, 11th August, 1932.
MITFORD, MARY RUSSELL, Our Village, 1824–1832, essay, A Great Farmhouse.
REW, R. H., Agricultural Tenancies in England. International Review of Agricultural Economics, April–June 1926.
STIRLING, A. M. W., Coke of Norfolk, and his friends, 1912.
SURTEES, R. L., Hillingdon Hall or the Cockney Squire, ed. of 1931.
WHITE, GILBERT, Natural History of Selborne, 1789.
WILLS, BARCLAY, Shepherds of Sussex, n.d., c. 1933.
WORDSWORTH, DOROTHY, Journal ed. by William Knight, Vol. I, 1897.

Authorities for Chapter Six

ANON., Farm Life, or sketches from the Country, 1861.
ANON., The Farmer and his Family, 1885.
BENNETT, ARNOLD, Anna of the Five Towns, 1902
BLOMEFIELD, MATHENA, The Bullemung Pit, 1944.
BLOMEFIELD, MATHENA, Nuts in the Rookery, 1946.
CLAPHAM, J. H., Economic History of Modern Britain, Vol. II. Free Trade and Steel, 1850–1886.
CLARKE, SIR ERNEST, The Foundation of the Royal Agricultural Society, Jour. R.A.S.E., 1890.
COMPTON, THEODORE, Winscombe; Sketches of Rural Life and Scenery amongst the Mendip Hills, 1882.
CROSSING, WILLIAM, A Hundred Years on Dartmoor, 5th ed., 1902.
DEVENISH, DOROTHY, A Wiltshire Country Home, 1948.
DONALDSON, J., British Agriculture, 1866.
FARMER, A., Wet Days, 1879.
GASKILL, MRS., Cousin Phyllis and other tales, 1865.
GOULD, BARING, Old Country Life, 1895.
GRETTON, M. STURGE, A Corner of the Cotswolds, 1914.
HOWITT, WILLIAM, Rural Life of England, 1838.
JEFFERIES, RICHARD, Hodge and his Masters, 1880.
JEFFERIES, RICHARD, My Old Vicarage, 1887.
JEFFERIES, RICHARD, The Toilers of the Field, ed. of 1894.
KEBBEL, T. E., The Old and the New English Country Life, 1891.
KENDALL, S. G., Farming Memoirs of a West Country Yeoman, 1945.
MASSINGHAM, H. J., A Countryman's Journal. *The Field*, 24th Nov., 1945.
Norfolk Clergyman, The Country Parish, 1852.
PEEL, HON. MRS. C. S., A Hundred Wonderful Years, 1820–1920, 1926.
Poet of the People, Anti-Maud, 1856.

PUSEY, PHILIP, On the farming of Lincolnshire, Jour. R.A.S.E., 1843.

Richmond Commission on Agriculture, 1879–1882.

SALTER, H. B., A Hundred Harvests Ago. *Farmers Weekly*, 6th Dec., 1946.

SAVORY, ARTHUR H., Grain and Chaff from an English Manor, 1920.

SHAND, ALEX. INNES, Half a Century; or changes in men and manners, 1887.

SHELDON, JOHN PRINCE, The Future of British Agriculture, 1893.

THOMPSON, EDWARD G., Men of Branber, 1944.

WARD, R. E., Life on a Dorset Farm. *Farmers Weekly*, 4th Oct., 1946.

WALKER, ELDRED F., Small farming at the beginning of the 20th century. Jour. Bath and West Soc., 4th Ser., XII, 1901–1902.

WATSON, J. A. SCOTT AND ELLIOT, MAY, Great Farmers, 1937.

WATSON, J. A. SCOTT, History of the Royal Agricultural Society of England, 1839–1939, 1939.

WINGFIELD-STRATFORD, ESME, Victorian Sunset, 1939.

YOUNG, G. M., ed. Early Victorian England, 1830–1865, 1934.

INDEX

A

B